ISLAM AND INDIAN MUSLIMS

ISLAM AND INDIAN MUSLIMS

Mir Sajjad Ali,
Zainab Rahman

KALPAZ

Islam and Indian Muslism

Rs. 750

ISBN: 978-81-7835-805-5

Published in 2010 in India by
Kalpaz Publications
C-30, Satyawati Nagar,
Delhi-110052
E-mail: kalpaz@hotmail.com
Phone : 9212729499

Lasser Type Setting by: Quick Media, Delhi
Printed at : Young Art Press, Delhi

Dedicated to My Husband and Children Who constitute My Life

CONTENTS

Foreword

All Religions, taken in their broadest sense aim at improving a human being to reach the highest level of nobility and purity of mind. Since the beginning of human history religion has in its various manifestations dominated man's conscious efforts. When guided by positive motivation, it imparted a healing touch to society. Conversely, a confrontationist approach creates violent social upheavals engendering prejudices and animosities. But the bonding elements of religion emanating from the spirituality of religions, override and nullify the diverse influence cast by their ritual Practices. That explains Voltaire's witticism "if god didn't exist, man would have to invent him". In the words of a Sufi saint, 'there is one religion, the unswerving progress in the right direction towards the ideal, which, fulfils the life's purpose of every soul. Further, that "our god and your god is one and it is to him that we bow". This book shows through Quaranic quotations that all religions are basically the same and hence should unite humanity rather than divide it. I feel this book will go a long way in clearing misconceptions and ignorance about Quranic teachings and contribute towards mutual understandings and respect among people of various faiths. "Bring to remembrance the benefits you have received from Allah and refrain from evil and mischief on the earth."

The authors, Mir Sajjad Ali and Zainab Rahman have put in great efforts have to compile Quarnic quotations under different heads like unity of religion, relevance of Quran in modern times, Quarnic views about women, marriage and family, Jehad and so on.

I knew Mir Sajjad Ali very well. He was a senior bureaucrat in the government of Andhra Pradesh at the time of his superannuation. His knowledge and expertise were gratefully acknowledged and appreciated by the different governments under which he served. He was a man of character and integraty who was also very warm hearted. He showered his love and affection on me generously. May his soul rest in peace. Amen

I am happy that his daughter, Zainab Rahman has incorporated his research on Quarnic quotations into her own work and produced this book. It is an absorbing and thought provoking book. It challenges some of our current conventional wisdom and forces us to think and reexamine comforting illusions about religion, clearing the way for a desirable era based on the bed-rock of religious morality. I wish the book all success.

Abid Hussain

Former Ambassador of India to U.S.A

Preface

As a Muslim I feel it is my duty to try and present the positive aspects of my religion in front of the world so that it may be appreciated properly. Unfortunately in recent times Islam has been in the news for all the wrong reasons. Even earlier, in the words of Bernard Shaw, 'Islam is the best religion but Muslims are the worst people'; Muslims have gathered a lot of flak. This shows that somewhere Muslims have been unsuccessful in presenting the true picture of their religion to the world. So it becomes all the more essential to clarify misconceptions and doubts not only in the minds of non Muslims but also the Muslims. It is true that quite a few Muslims do not know much about their religion and worst still they believe in various wrong concepts and follow many wrong customs in the name of Islam. With such rampant ignorance prevailing it is a daunting task to present the facts, but I am determined to try to do it. May Allah help and guide me in my endeavour. It is ironic that while the literal meaning of the word Islam is Peace, today it is equated with violence and terror by many. This sad state of affairs is the result of many historic and political events and it is not only the Muslims who are to be blamed for it. Muslims were killed, ill treated and discriminated against in different parts of the world in different ways in the last hundred years and finally some of them have decided to resort to extreme violence to avenge themselves. Of course the method they have adopted is wrong and these acts of terrorism cannot be called Jehad. The true meaning of Jehad and conditions laid down for Jehad will be discussed in detail in a separate chapter, but here I would like to mention that while Muslims have to take the initiative to improve themselves in order to influence world conditions positively others also have to cooperate, and help in achieving peace and goodwill.

The idea of writing this book also took shape when I came to know that my late father, a very learned and devout Muslim, had compiled many quotations from the Holy Quran under the headings of Islam, the universal religion, unity of all religions and the relevance of Islam in modern times. He was a very modest man and did not feel that his efforts were worthy of publication, but I felt that they should be published so that the right message is put across to the world. Incidentally, my research was about Islam and social change among Muslims and for the last two decades I have been writing about Islam and specially Muslim women. It's a coincidence that recently I presented a paper about relevance of Islam for the modern man at a National Seminar and the paper was published in a book to commemorate the Seminar. When I got the notes from my elder brother, that my father had made, I was compelled to take up this project, which had always been there in my mind anyway. In this book I have quoted extensively from the Quran in order to give authentic information about various issues. Quoting from the Quran will provide the real knowledge about Islam which alas very few possess. The first four chapters are based mainly on the quotations compiled by my father, late Mir Sajjad Ali, with a few extra ones that I found relevant. The other chapters are based mainly on my research on Quranic quotations, with some inputs from the quotations collected by Abba. The views expressed are mine and since my father is not alive, I cannot get his opinion on them; but I have a feeling that he might have held similar views. This is only a conjecture and hence I am solely responsible for the views expressed. Explanation and interpretation is a difficult job and can lead to misunderstanding and misrepresentation, therefore I have tried to rely on the explanations given by non controversial and emminent scholars as far as possible and tried to express my views also in a logical and moderate way. My main aim is to bring about goodwill among all people. I hope God will help me to achieve this objective and I do not create any misunderstandings or ill will among the readers.

I feel at this stage I must introduce my father to the readers as he is a co author of this book. My father, Mir Sajjad Ali belonged to Hyderabad. He was the youngest son in a respectable and intellectual family. Both his parents were highly educated and interested in literature and religion. Both were fond of writing and contributed to literary magazines. A collection of my grandfather's poetry in praise of Prophet Mohammad PBUH was published by my uncle some years back. Abba [as we adressed our father] used to say that all the literary Urdu he knew was mostly learnt by listening to the conversations and discusions of his parents. Their discussions also gave him a thirst for knowledge and linguistics. Unfortunately Abba lost his parents when he was about nine years old. He was brought up by his eldest brother who was much older than him. He was a brilliant student both at school and college. He topped in Mathematics in BA at the Nizam College Hyderabad. He was offered a seat at Oxford but could not avail of the opportunity due to financial reasons. He appeared for the Hyderabad Civil Service Exam. And topped in it receiving a Gold Medal. At the young age of 23 years he was appointed an under secretary in the Secratariat of the Government of Hyderabad under the Nizam's rule. After independence there was a lot of trouble in Hyderabad as the Indian Government resorted to Police Action in Sept 1948 to annex the Hyderabad state to The Indian Union. The Muslim officers suffered a lot and many resigned from service. Abba did not, although he fell ill and suffered financial difficulties. Later on he was appointed the Joint Secretary Finance to the Andhra Pradesh Government in which capacity he served for many years with deputation postings at other offices. He was a very conscientious and honest officer and was highly respected for his integrity and unbending principles. After retirement he worked as Comptroller Andhra Pradesh Agricultural University for three years. He was a fun loving person and enjoyed socialising with his friends. He was very popular with his colleagues. He was a good bridge player and spent long hours mastering new techniques and playing in tournaments. He was also a good homeopath and treated all of us from minor ailments. He was a very good father and husband. We all had a very happy family life.

He was a devout Muslim but never made a show of religosity. He tried to follow all important tenets of Islam with out making a fuss. He taught us Quran Sharef at night and discussed various religious matters with us but he never was dogmatic either in his views or in the guidance he gave us. He was a secular person in the sense that he had friends of all religions and enjoyed all festivals and was a patriotic Indian. He always taught us that as Indians we have pledged to be loyal to our country and as Muslims it is our duty to keep this promise always because Muslims have been enjoined to keep their promises at all costs. He encouraged us to make friends with all children and take part in all activities at school. He never preached but set a good example for us to follow. He was not rigid and disliked a fanatic approach to religion. I feel that thanks to his guidance we brothers and sisters made very good progress in life and are good citizens. He also taught us that merit always wins and so we should do our best and wait for good results. He never encouraged us to feel that we would be discriminated against for any reason and probably this positive attitude has really helped us. I have made a special mention of this because generally Muslims have a feeling that they are being discriminated against and sometimes it is also true. There is discrimination at various levels. On our part we can only do our best and develop a positive attitude. It is also the duty of others not to discriminate on the basis of religion or even caste and sex, as it is wrong. But if right vibrations are sent to others they may desist from discriminating. This is purely my personal opinion which may or may not be correct.

In India there are many problems today and people of all religions and creeds face them. The Government tries to solve the problems but is not fully successful. The people have to make their own efforts in the right direction to achieve their goals. Generally we resort to wrong means because unfortunately in our country corruption flourishes in every sphere and people cant resist the temptation to take the short cut instead of working hard and honestly. This applies to all Indians. We have to try and be honest and hard working and judge according to merit. Only then can we have social justice and contentment among different sections of the population. Muslims should also strive to compete with everyone else and take their rightful place in the affairs of the nation. Although in recent times injustice may have been done to some Muslims, they should not lose heart, instead they should try to prove their potential and be successful against all odds. We have the example of those Muslims in Gujarat, who are fighting against all odds and an unjust rule, to continue their lives successfully, but most of the poor Gujarati Muslims are still suffering and the authorities are doing nothing to reduce then suffering, as written by Bitta Ohm in EPW of Dec. 8-14, 2007. Muslims of India, belong only to India. It is their homeland. No one can oust them. They have the same rights as other citizens but they also have same duties and obligations too. Those Muslims who have faced discrimination are bound to feel hurt and might tend to react violently. This is not a healthy attitude as it aggravates the situation rather than set it right. On the other hand it is not right to keep on tolerating injustice. The correct thing to do is to retaliate through legitimate means allowed in a democracy, like protest march, signature campaign, representation and legal action, although in our country all these means are ridden with inefficiency and corruption. Secondly Muslims should aim at increasing their capabilities and assets so that it becomes nearly impossible for others to discriminate, specially in academics and employment.

This book is an attempt to present the teachings and contents of Quran which are relevant to modern times and which substantiate the authors' surmise that all religions are one and The Supreme Power is One whom different people worship by different names. Only Quranic quotations will be presented to maintain authenticity and avoid controversies. Controversies arise only when different interpretations are drawn from any sacred text, be it of any religion. The author aims to use references of highly acclaimed authorities on religion who have explained things clearly, in an unambigous way. Since the author [Zainab Rahman] is a student and teacher of Sociology, she has given a sociological bend to her explanations and reasoning sometimes. Sociology says that religion is a social phenomenon, while it has become politically correct to say that religion is a personal matter. The author feels that the former opinion is correct because all religions are ways of life and are practised by people in groups as members of a larger society. Of course it is essential to coexist peacefully so there should be tolerance and some common meeting points theoretically and practically, but religious practices will continue to involve the whole group, rather than only the individual. Individuals will have to be careful in practising their traditions in such a way that they do not intrude on others and do not hurt anyone. Although we sometimes have problems in our country, by and large, the tolerance and peaceful co existance found in such a highly plural society like India is exemplary and should be followed by other societies.

Since this book is based mainly on Quranic quotations, the Tranlation referred to are important. In the first four chapters, which are based mainly on the work done by Mir Sajjad Ali, the translation used is by Mohammad Marmaduke Pickthall. Some quotations which have been added by Zainab Rahman are from the translation by NJ Dawood. In later chapters translations of Hilali& Mohsin Khan as well as translation by Abdullah Yusuf Ali have been used. Generally the translations were all similar, but if there was some ambiguity then other translations were also consulted and the most appropriate, according to the author was used. At the end of each chapter, the translations referred to have been mentioned.

Acknowledgements

I am very happy that I was able to complete this book, which was a very cherished dream for me. I wanted to present the work that my late father, Mr. Mir Sajjad Ali had done by collecting quotations from the Quran about unity of religions, the relevance of Quranic teachings in modern times and Islam as the universal religion. I have added my own research on Quranic quotations about some other important issues which also have contemporary significance. The Quran encourages all its readers to ponder on its teachings and learn from them. Allah promises to help those who are sincerely interested in understanding, to arrive at correct conclusions. [Surah 54 verse 40] Hence I made this effort with the sincere hope that Allah will help me understand and express in the correct way.

I am grateful to Dr Abid Hussain, Former Indian Ambassador to USA, for writing an inspiring Foreword to my book. He knew my father personally so I was very keen that he write about him. I am really thankful to him for obliging me in this respect. I am thankful to my brother who made the manuscript written by my father available to me and to my sister who helped through my writing of the book in many ways. I am thankful to all those at my workplace who helped me. Finally I am grateful to my husband and my children for giving me moral support and many other type of help during my work. Thanks to everyone's efforts and good wishes the book is finally ready and I hope will be well received.

Zainab Rahman

1

Introduction

Islam is one of the major religions of the world which has followers in all parts of the world. The literal meaning of Islam is Peace and submission to the Will of Allah, the followers of Islam are Muslims. Quran is the holy book of the Muslims. Muslims believe it is the Word of Allah, revealed to Prophet Mohammad. Prophet Mohammad was born in Arabia in the 6th century AD. At the age of 40 years Allah chose him as the last prophet to be sent to humanity to teach them the Eternal Truth which was revealed to all earlier prophets of Allah at different times and places. Prophet Mohammad started preaching to the people of Mecca and the rest of Arabia, and later to the people of different countries about the Truth as revealed to him in the Holy Quran.

Islam spread rapidly, both during the life time of the Prophet and soon after during the Khilafat of the earliest Khalifas. Today, Islam is the principal religion of much of Asia and the Middle East. Major Muslim countries are Indonesia [with the world's largest Muslim population], Malaysia, Pakistan, Bangladesh, Afghanistan, Azarbaijan, Uzbekistan, Turkmenistan, Tajakistan, Kyrgystan, Iraq, Iran, Syria, Jordan, Saudi Arabia and other Arab penensula states, and Turkey. India also has one of the largest Muslim populations in the world although Islam is not the principal religion there. In Africa, Islam is the principal religion in Egypt Algeria, Tunisia, Mauritania, Morocco, Niger, Senegal, Mali, Gambia, Somalia and Sudan, with sizable populations in Nigeria, Ethiopia, Ghana, Eritrea, Chad and Tanzania. In Europe Albania is predominantly Muslim. Historically Bulgaria, Bosnia, Macedonia and Georgia have had Muslim populations. Spain was under Muslim rule for centuries. Today Muslim immigrant communities from North Africa, Turkey and Asia are found in France, Germany, Great Britain and other countries. There are increasing numbers of European converts to Islam. In America too, Islamic population has substantially increased in recent times both from conversions and immigrations from other parts of the world. Islam is considered the third monotheistic world religion along with its predecessors Christianity and Judaism. These three religions have a lot in common not only in their content but also in their historic background. In fact, the Holy book of the Muslims, the Quran, which was revealed to Prophet Mohammad PBUH by Allah says many times that the patriarch Abraham who is revered by Jews, Christians and Muslims, was a Muslim, because he had surrendered himself completely to the Will of Allah. Thus Quran preaches unity of all religions and proclaims Islam as the universal religion. Prophet Mohammad was sent to remind the people of Allah's teachings for a final time through Allah's word in the form of the Holy Quran. He was sent to Arabia because no prophet had come to the Arabs and they had not been guided for a long long time.

The term Muslim world has several meanings. In a cultural sense it refers to the world wide community of Muslims, adherents of Islam. This community numbers about 1. 5 to 2 billion people, about one fourth of the world. It is spread across many different nations and ethnic groups connected only by religion. In a historical or geopolitical sense the term usually refers collectively to countries with Muslim majority or countries in which Islam dominates politically. The world wide Muslim community is also known as the Ummah. Islam emphasises unity of Ummah and defence of fellow Muslims although many divisions [like Shia Sunni] exist in Islam. In the past both Pan Islamism and national current have influenced the status of the Muslim world. [Internet]

The Quran was revealed to Prophet Mohammad by Allah through the Angel Gabriel. It is a literary masterpiece and the very fact that it was recited to the Arab world by an unlettered Prophet proves that it is a Divine revelation. It is the last comprehensive message from God through the last Prophet to the entire human race. Allah has promised to protect the Quran for ever. "It was We that revealed the Quran and shall Ourself preserve it. " Surah XV verse 9 and 'You [Mohammad] need not move your tongue too fast to learn this revelation. We Ourself shall see to its collection and recital. When We read it, follow its words attentively; We shall Ourself explain its meaning' [Surah 75. Verses 16 – 18] The Quran explains the basic tenets of Islam, the universal religion, as follows: Iman [belief in One God, Day of Judgement, The Holy books, Prophets and Angels], Namaz, Roza, Zakat and Haj. These have been enjoined upon believers in the following verses:

Surah 2 verse 285 'The Apostle believes in what has been revealed to him by his Lord, and so do the faithful. They all believe in Allah and His angels, His scriptures, and His apostles : We discriminate against none of His apostles. They say:' We hear and obey. Grant us your forgiveness, Lord; to You we shall all return.'

Surah 2 verse 238 'Attend regularly to your prayers, including the middle prayer, and stand up with all devotion before Allah.'

Surah 2 verse 267 'Believers, give in alms of the wealth you have lawfully earned and of that which We have brought out of the earth for you;'

Surah 2 verse 183 'Believers, fasting is decreed for you as it was decreed for those before you; perchance you will guard yourselves against evil.'

Surah 2 verse 196 'Make the Pilgrimage and visit the Sacred House [Kaaba] for His sake.' These orders have been repeated in many other verses too. If we ponder over these basic tenets we will notice that they are universal in the sense that in every religion followers have been ordained to believe in The Supreme Being, obey Him and perform prayers, fast, give alms and perform pigrimage of holy places. Of course there may be some variations in the details.

The Quran gives detailed accounts of events right from the creation of the universe, right up to the future when Allah will raise the dead from their graves on the Day of Judgement. The beauty of the Quran is expressed thus by Allah, 'Perfected is the Word of thy Lord in truth and justice. There is naught that can change His words. He is the Hearer, the Knower.' [Surah 6 verse 115] and "Allah has now revealed the best of scriptures, a book uniform in style proclaiming promises and warnings Those who fear their Lord are filled with awe as they listen to its revelations, so that their hearts soften at the rememberance of Allah. Such is Allah's guidance : He bestows it on whom He will. But he whom Allah misleads shall have none to guide him." [Surah 39 verse 23] Allah tells the prophet to tell the people who do not believe in the Quran, 'Say: The Holy Spirit brought it down from your Lord in truth to reassure the faithful, and to give guidance and good news to those that surrender themselves to Allah.' [Surah 16 verse 102] Allah confirms that the Quran is His Word in the following quotation, "This Quran could not have been composed by any but Allah. It confirms what was revealed before it and fully explains the Scriptures. It is beyond doubt from the Lord of the Creation" [Surah 10 verse 37] Allah also explains why the Quran was sent in stages. "The unbelievers ask: Why was the Quran not revealed to him entire in a single revelation? We have revealed it thus so that We may strengthen your faith. We have imparted it to you by gradual revelation. No sooner will they come to you with an argument than We shall reveal to you the truth and properly explain it." [Surah 25 verses 32, 33] While the above verses of the Quran, and many others express the good qualities of this divine revalation and give proof of its being a divine revalation, they also show that it is not confined to only one period of time or to people of one particular region, because it gives details of different prophets and regions and different times in human history and fortells about the Day of Judgement when all humans will be raised from the dead and judged for their actions. Thus it is the Word of the Lord of all creation and is addressed to the entire mankind. A common misconception among non-believers has been that Quran is not the Word of God but written by Prophet Mohammad. This is an absurd concept because Prophet Mohammad could not read or write and the Quran is a masterpiece of Arabic literature. Secondly, the Quran proclaims again and again that it is the Word of God and challenges non believers to write similar verses if they can. In this connection, besides the quotations already given, the following quotations are also relevant:

> Surah 56 verse 77- 80 'I swear by the shelter of the stars [a mighty oath, if you but knew it] that this is a glorious Quran, inscribed in a hidden book which none may touch except the purified; a revelation from the Lord of all creatures. Would you scorn a scripture such as this and make it your daily task to deny it?'

Surah 17 verse 88 'Say : 'If men and jinn combined to write the like of this Quran, they would surely fail to compose one like it, though they helped one another.'

In many other verses people have been challenged to produce even one verse similar to Quranic verses, if they can and Allah has also proclaimed that they can't. Allah says again and again that the truth has been revealed so whoso wants to believe can do so and Allah will guide him, but whoso wants to disbelieve and make fun of Allah's Word will not understand and Allah too would leave him in darkness. Even Prophet Mohammad has been told again and again that he is only a messenger and he cannot force anyone to believe; only those will believe who are sincerely interested in finding the truth and Allah will guide them. After this there is no point in arguing with anyone if they do not believe that Quran is the Word of God.

The Quran is universally accepted as written with purity of language and in an elegant style It is a masterpiece of literary production. It is admirable in its concept of divine nature, its fervent trust is the power of one God and its deep moral earnestness and its sententious wisdom It is a standard of the Arabic language. Its style is beautiful and fluent, and when prophesying it soars higher.[1] N J Dawood writes, the Quran is the earliest and by far the finest work of Classical Arabic prose. For Muslims it is the infallible word of God, a transcript of a tablet preserved in Heaven, revealed to the Prophet Mohammad by the Angel Gabriel. Except in the opening verses and some few passages in which the Prophet or the Angel speaks in the first person, the speaker through out is God. The Quran preaches the oneness of God and emphasises divine mercy and forgiveness. God is Almighty and All knowing and though compassionate towards His creatures He is stern in retribution. He enjoins justice and fair dealing, kindness to orphans and widows, charity to the poor. The most important duties of the Muslim are faith in Allah and His apostle, prayer, almsgiving, fasting and [if possible] pilgrimage to the Sacred House at Mecca, built by Abraham for the worship of the One God. [2]

In his book, Calling to Islam, Imran rightly writes, "The word ISLAM means The Way of Peaceful Surrender to the Will of Almighty, Allah. Many people have a misconception that Islam was introduced to the mankind by the Last Prophet of Allah, Mohammad [pbuh], but the Quran says "This day have We completed your religion for you" [Surah 5 verse 3] which shows that Islam was not introduced to prophet Mohammad [pbuh] about 1425 years back instead Prophet Mohammad came to complete the teachings of Islam." The Quran has 114 chapters of unequal length called Suras. These are divided into verses. Each Sura is headed by a special title, Some of these chapters have been revealed by stages during a period of twenty three years over which the rvelations of the Holy book are spread. [3] Some quotations of learned non Muslims about the Quran and the Prophet Mohammad are as follows:

> 'The Quran is an incomparable code of guidance whose teachings are in accordance with human nature.' John Davenport in History of the World.

'There has been no other book in the last fourteen hundred years which has been revered and followed as meticulously as the Holy Quran.' William Moore

'Even if a non Muslim follows the teachings of Quran, he can make great progress.' German Professor Hogg.

'Prophet Mohammad was a high level political thinker and he set up a political system which was excellent.' Rousseau

Many Muslim scholars have also written about the qualities and teachings of the Quran. Sir Syed Ahmad Khan, the great Muslim reformer had written a lot about the Quran and its message to humanity. In his book, The Destiny of Indian Muslims, S Abid Husain writes, 'Sir Syed was convinced that true Islamic teaching and Islamic life were in perfect harmony with reason and 'nature'and could meet the legitimate demands of every age. According to him, Muslims had however, in the course of centuries, deviated from true Islam and their faith and practice had become encumbered with a number of accretions which had nothing to do with Islamic teachings. It was necessary to get rid of these accretions and to go back to the essence of the religion which could be found in its authentic form only in the Quran. He believed in genuine traditions of the Prophet [hadith] as clarification of the Quranic injunctions, but did not accept the opinion of any single jurist [faqih] or the consensus of juritic opinion [ijma] as binding, and 'in questions that have not been specifically dealt with in the Quran or Hadith' he allowed every Muslim the right of personal interpretation in the light of the Quran'. In this regard the following quotations from the Quran support the idea of thinking for one's self about Allah's Word and not refuting it with out reason or even having blind faith, 'The meanest beasts in Allah's sight are those that are deaf, dumb and devoid of reason.' [Surah 8 verse 22] showing that God wants people to reason and ponder about the Word of God and then believe in it; and 'Those who do not fall as blind and deaf on the revelations of their Lord when they are reminded of them.' [Surah 25 vere 73] has been related as a sign of true servants of God, showing the importance of using one's reason to understand the Word of God Another quotation which denounces people who do not ponder is as follows: Surah 7 verse 179 'Many are the Jinns and men We have made for Hell. They have hearts wherewith they understand not, eyes wherewith they see not; and ears wherewith they hear not. They are like cattle—nay more misguided; for they are heedless.' These quotations support Sir Syed's view that we should ponder on the meaning of the Holy Book and try to understand to the best of our capability. Thus, according to his above mentioned principles, Sir Syed wrote thought provoking articles in his journal *Tahzib ul Akhlaq* on a number of major and minor religious matters. He started a commentary of the Quran but could not complete it. The fundamental principle which he followed in his commentary is that the Word of God [Quran] must be in harmony with the Work of God [Nature]. The Quran consists of two kinds of verses, Mohkamat which have a clear precise meaning and Mutashabihat which convey the idea in metaphorical language. The verse of the latter kind can have no definite and final interpretation, valid for all time. As the knowledge and experience of man increases and he gets a clearer perception of the world of nature, deeper meanings of these verses will be revealed to him and he will give them new interpretations. In this regard the following quotation from the Quran itself is relevent here. "It is He who has revealed to you the Quran. Some of its verse are precise in meaning - they are the foundation of the Book –and others ambiguous. Those whose hearts are infected with disbelief follow the ambiguous part, so as to create dissension by seeking to explain it But no one knows its meaning except Allah. Those who are well grounded in knowledge say : We believe in it: it is all from our Lord. " [Surah 3 verse 7]

The fundamental ideas underlying Sir Syed's attempt at religious reforms are:

1. In religious thought and practice it is not enough to follow established authority. Every age requires a fresh interpretation according to the needs of time.
2. To make Islamic teachings intelligible and acceptable to the whole of humanity, it is necessary to express them in rational terms.[4] He worked towards this end through out his life.

According to the Quran Islam is the universal religion which was preached by all the apostles of God. Islam is not only a religion, it is a way of life just like Hinduism too is a way of life. In fact all religions are actually ways of leading a good life. This means that Islam not only teaches how to pray and how to achieve salvation but also teaches about daily life, about social institutions, social conduct, social relationships, matters of the world like property rights, business transactions, social values and so on. In fact every apostle taught his followers about good conduct and social responsibilities and all these are finally repeated in Quran which is the final Word of God. At the same time every apostle also warned about bad behaviour and its consequences, which again was also done by prophet Mohammad through the Quran. In this connection the following quotation from

Prof. Mujeeb's book appears relevant here. He writes, 'The first question every Muslim must ask himelf today is whether he really regard Islam as a universal religion or only as the religion of those that call themselves Muslims. The theological statement, based on the authority of the Quran, is that the true faith has been revealed to all mankind through prophets, not all of whom have been mentioned in the Quran by name. But the peoples to whom the true faith was revealed have deviated from it, the deviations of the Jews and the Christians specially being commented upon in the Quran. Muslims feel they are rightly guided and will be forgiven and surely sent to heaven but they forget the conditions that are almost always attached of sincere belief and performance of good deeds whenever any thing is said in the Quran about believers and Muslims. It is also forgotten that the Quran mentions there are believers also among the Ahl Kitab, but Muslims do believe in universalism of Islam. We may conclude that Islam is a universal faith revealed by God to all mankind, that the Quran is, as it says 'an exposition for mankind and a guidance, and an admonition for such as are God fearing, and the verse 'We try you with good and evil for a testing, then unto Us you shall be returned'[Quran: 80: 34-37] is addressed to all humanity not only Muslims. If Islam is a universal religion, and among mankind are those who believe, those who only profess to believe and those who do not believe at all in the one God and His guidance, all problems should be considered not in the light of Islamic theology and history only but in the context of world hitory. We must study the history of all religions to see how close they are in essence to the fundamental human faith.[5]

The Quran gives detailed instructions about all the matters related to daily life and conduct and aims at teaching its reader the proper way of leading an honest and good life which will bring happiness and contentment both in this world and in the Hereafter. According to the Quran, Allah has sent down the same instructions through all prophets right from the time of Adam to Prophet Mohammad, though the rituals and Shariat [code of conduct] differed from nation to nation, because of changed conditions and times. According to Quran the true religion is one and in Arabic it is given the name AL ISLAM which means surrender to the will of the Creator. Thus all the religions which were revealed to different prophets are basically one and Mohamad is the last prophet of ISLAM. The Quran gives detailed accounts of the Prophets Adam, Noah, Abraham, Moses, Jesus, David, Solomon, Jonas and many others again and again. The Quran does not relate the story of the early years of Prophet Mohammad's life in such detail as it does of Abraham, Ismael Moses, Joseph and Jesus. This clearly shows it is a Holy book for followers of all religions. About Prophet Mohammad the Quran says he is the last prophet of Allah and he is a blessing and benevolent guide for the entire humanity. The Quran exhorts the Prophet again and again to continue with his preaching without any fear and to overlook all the inconveniences and abuses heaped on him by the non believers just as Allah's other messengers had done before him. Allah also promises to protect His messenger from the evil designs of his enemies, and says that Allah always helps the good and upright.

Here it is neccessary to explain clearly that the Quran testifies all the previous religions and prophets as true, but it also says that with time the followers of each religion have introduced some wrong notions into their religious practices which should be corrected. Today we see that the Muslims also have introduced many wrong customs and notions in their religious beliefs and practices. The erroneous concept that Muslims feel that only their faith is right and all other faiths are not right is so widespread that it has caused a lot of ill will and problems. Many Muslims continue to believe it, which is not right. The Quran says again and again that all those who believe in One Supreme Being and the day of

Judgement and do good will be rewarded. No human being is capable of judging another human being on this account. Recently the author came across an opinion of a non-Muslim, in the Time of India, that since prophet Mohammad [pbuh] told his followers to proclaim Kalma Tayyaba, i.e. 'there is no god but Allah and Mohammad is His prophet', Muslims have become intolerant of other faiths and resort to violence against others. This again is an incorrect statement. In fact the Quran tells Muslims not to speak ill of other faiths or their deities. 'Revile not those unto whom they pray beside Allah lest they wrongfully revile Allah through ignorance. Thus unto every nation have We made their deed seem fair'[Surah 6 verse 108]When the prophet asked his followers to proclaim unity of Allah, he meant the One Supreme Being in whom people of all religions believe. In the next chapter we will deal in detail with the concept of One Supreme Being in all religions. The thesis presented by the Quran is that all religions are the same and in Arabic the name of this universal religion is AL ISLAM and the Supreme Being is ALLAH. If we stop to ponder, the original name of Hinduism is Sanatan Dharma which means true religion and the word ued for Supreme Being is OM. It is quite logical to believe that this ancient religion was preached by some earlier mesenger of the same Supreme Being who has sent His message to different peoples at different times. The basic message is always the same, which we can notice in the main teachings of all world religions.

The Quran also conveys the same message. It repeats many injunctions and teachings again and again to impress upon its readers the importance of them. All major Surahs, in fact are quite comprehensive in themselves and mention all important issues either in detail or in passing. Some topics which have been oft repeated in the Quran are as follows: the creation of the universe and first man, Adam, the Day of Judgement, and description of Heaven and Hell, stories of earlier prophets specially Abraham, Moses and Jesus[who were given Scriptures] and also older ones like Adam, Noah, Saleh, Hud and later ones like Jacob, Joseph, David, Solomon, Job and Jonas. Allah says that many more prophets were sent about whom no one knows except Allah. The Quran also gives details of good behaviour and evil acts and exhorts men to do the former and desist from the latter. Jehad or fight against evil, rules of war, treatment of enemies and allies, observance of justice and mercy, maintaining a good character and leading a good family life, treatment of relatives, widows and orphans and many other worldly matters are discussed in the Quran.

It gives details of rules for marriage, divorce, care of children, treatment of fellow beings, property rights, business transactions, social evils and their harmful effects, rules of ettiquette and civilized behaviour, irrespective of religious orientation, and many other issues which are related to daily life. Thus it has relevance for the entire humanity and for all times.

The Quran announces many times that it is a Guide and Enlightenment for all mankind. It encourages people to read and understand the message of the Quran and seek divine help and guidance for proper understanding. God says often that those who are inclined towards learning the truth will be directed by God to follow the right path but those who are interested only in rediculing and refuting the truth will be left in darkness [ignorance] rather God will prevent them from understanding the truth due to their initial disbelief and depravity. However if such people repent truly and ask for God's guidance, they will surely receive it because God is ever Merciful and Kind. Allah tells prophet Mohammad in the Quran, 'We have revealed to you the Book with the truth, for the instruction of mankind. He that follows the right path shall follow it to his own advantage; and he that goes astray sshall do so at his own peril. You are not accountable for them' [Surah 39 verse 41]

Right from the beginning the Quran makes it clear that all the commandments are for those who believe in God and fear Him. 'Alif lam mim. This book is not to be doubted It is a guide for the righteous [God fearing], who have faith in the unseen and are steadfast in prayer; who bestow in charity a part of what We have given them; who trust what has been revealed to you [Mohammad] and to others before you, and firmly believe in the life to come. These are rightly guided by their Lord; these shall surely triumph.'Surah 2 verses 1- 4. Allah also tells the prophet that he can only preach and offer guidance but he cannot make people believe; only those who are so inclined and capable of comprehending the truth will believe. Allah judges people according to their inclinations and actions and then guides those who seek the truth diligently. 'And whomsoever it is God's Will to guide, He expandeth his bosom unto the Surrender and whomsoever it is His Will to send astray, He maketh his bosom close and narrow as if he were engaged in sheer ascent [climbing] Thus Allah layeth ignominy upon those who believe not.' [Surah 6 verse125] The Quran describes all the small and big wonders of Nature which are the Work of God in order to exlain the greatness and omnipotence of God to the people and it admonishes them again and again to think and ponder and learn from what they see and experience around them and in their own lives. Time and again the Quran exhorts people to ponder about the happenings in nature and realise the meticulous management and direction of the Almighty of the entire universe. 'He has forced the night and the day, and the sun and the moon, into your service : the stars also serve you by His leave. Surely in this there are signs for men of undertanding. On the earth He has fashioned for you objects of various hues: surely in this there is a sign for prudent men.' Surah 16 verse 12 & 13 and after mentioning more about various other creations Allah asks, 'Is He, then who has wrought the creation, like him who has created nothing? Will you not take heed?' [Surah 16 vere 17] Once again in Surah Rome Allah encourages people to observe and ponder as follows: "He gave you wives from among yourselves, that you might live in joy with them, and planted love and kindness in your hearts. Surely there are signs in this for thinking people. By another sign of His you sleep at night and seek by day His bounty. Surely there are signs in this for those who hear. He sends down water from the sky and with it He quickens the dead earth. Surely in this there are signs for men of understanding. " [Surah 30: verses 21- 24] Another verse of similar meaning is [38:29 "Here is a Book which we have sent down unto thee, full of blessings, that they may meditate on its signs, and that men of understanding may receive admonition."] On the other hand Allah denounces the people who do not think about Allah's message and do not observe the Works of Allah carefully, in order they believe, as quoted earlier [Surah 7 verse 179] Thus the Quran tells us that those who want can benefit through it, by reading it with understanding and genuine interest, and those who are initially perverted will not believe in it.

The Quran is thus a guide, a light and a blessing for the entire mankind as it is the final message from the Almighty and confirms all earlier scriptures that were sent by Almighty. As mentioned earlier, the apostle to whom it was revealed, Prophet Mohammad, has also been proclaimed a blessing for all humanity because he is the last prophet of the eternal religon of the Almighty. Allah tells mankind, 'Men, an admonition has come to you from your Lord, a healing ointment for your souls, a guide and a blessing to true believers.' [Surah 10 verse 57] In another verse Allah says, 'Thus We have revealed the Book to you [Mohammad]. Those to whom We gave the Scripture believe in it, and so do some of your own people. Only the unbelievers deny Our revelations. Never have you read a book before this, nor have you transcribed one with your right hand. Had you done either of these; the unbelievers might have justly doubted. But to those who are endowed with knowledge it is an undoubted sign. Only the wrongdoers deny Our signs.' [Surah 29, verses 47-48] There are many more verses which speak about the authenticity, divinity and universal appeal of the Quran and many others which challenge the non believers to produce even one verse like that of the Quran with the help of whoever they like; Allah says they will never be able to do so.

Thus in this chapter we have seen how Islam is the eternal religion which was preached by different names by different prophets and Quran is the final message of God which was sent through the last prophet of Islam, Prophet Mohammad pbuh.

References

1. Dawood NJ 1978 The Koran A Translation Allen Lane London.
2. Glimpses of World Religions published by JAICO Books 1957.
3. Imran 1978 Calling to Islam IREF Hyderabad.
4. S Abid Hussain 1965 The Destiny of Indian Muslims.
5. M Mujeeb 1972 Islamic Influence on Indian Society Meenakshi Prakashan.

Translations

1. Dawood NJ 1978 The Koran A Translation. Allen have London.
2. Mohd. M. Pickthall Holy Quran English Translation.

2

Islam, A Universal Religion : Unity of All Religions

Religion is defined as belief in the supernatural. Sociologically religious experience is intrinsic to the social phenomenon called religion. Though subjective, experience tends to be related to something external, material and non-material. It may be internal as well. Religious experience relates to something which is unempirical and non-material believed to be beyond this phenomenal world. That something is the supernatural of the sociologist. It is non human, super human all pervaive transcendental power like other forms of behaviour related to man's need, it is intrinsic part of man's existential baggage. By his very nature, man combines the world herein and the world hereafter. The super human belongs to the world hereafter. Religion takes birth when this experience enters into and expresses itself in man's institutionalised behaviour in the belief and practices related to the supernatural- and all this complex of phenomenon affects and shapes man's inter personal, intra group and inter group relationships with a strong sense of identity as related to the concepts and explanations of the conceived supernatural.

In the domain of religion, the monotheistic and monolithic concept, intellectually set in the civilizational framework of Semetism, stands face to face with the polytheism of the multiplicity of gods coupled with the worship of ghosts, spirits, material objects phenomena of Nature, with each phenomenon being governed by a god or gods and ancestor worship. In the latter concept gods and spirits were personal and anthropomorphised, as good as fellow human beings who by possessing selected males and \or females, would talk face to face with the person in distress and difficulty or needing emotional security and serenity, while in the monotheistic religions the Supernatural Power was male. It was omni present, omni potent and formless. Human eye cannot see it. Beyond this, in other concepts the Supernatural Power manifested itself in innumerable varied forms. This interface between the savage and the civilized, the sophisticated and the bizarre, turned the Europian thought to evolutionism as a methodology to study religion. This led to the search for origin of religion. Many alternatives like the concept of Soul, the ancestor\ghost worship, Animism and child like psychology of primitive man, fear and need for emotional security were considered as the origin of religion.[1] In Sociology a dichotomy of animism and monotheistic religions developed, but many thinkers also feel that there is a connection and continuance in the philosophy of primitive, polytheistic religions and the later monotheistic religions. The concept of unity of religions and a universal religion for the entire humankind is gaining ground among intellectuals of today, in the hope of bringing about peace and harmony in the world.

Maulana Azad has written a very comprehensive and lucid exposition of the Quranic message and teachings together with a detailed translation in Urdu, under the title Tarjumanul Quran. Since the Maulana had a mastery both over Arabic, his mother tongue, and Urdu, his translation is considered accurate. His explanations are also very logical and impartial. He has written about different religions of the world and tried to describe the evolution of human thought with regard to the Supernatural. He writes that though most ancient religions like Taoism of China and Hinduism of India, practised idol worship and were polytheistic, there was always the concept of one Supreme

Being in these religions which was above all other gods and goddesses; the intellectual elite realised that this Supreme Being alone was worth worshipping but the masses were allowed to satisfy their various childlike beliefs by worshipping local deities. In Iran Zorastra also preached belief in one Supreme Being, Ahur Mazda, rather than the prevalent belief in many gods, during his life time. Buddhism was a religion which developed basically as a protest to Brahminic superiority in Hinduism and did not present a concept of a Supreme Being at all, but after Buddha his followers started worshipping him as a god and built his idols profusely. Judaism, Christianity and Islam are monotheistic religions which have a lot in common in their teachings, beliefs and history. Thus the concept of one God has been prevalent in all religions and the words used for it have been similar like, Yahova, Ilahi, Eli or Allah. The Maulana also explains with Quranic quotations that the Quran does not claim to bring any new message to humanity but is repeating the same old message of Allah that was brought to humanity by earlier prophets. According to this message there is no God but Allah or Supreme Being. He will reward those who believe in Him and follow the right path and will punish those who do not believe in Him and follow the wrong path, on the Day of Judgement. This is because He has not created the whole universe with out a purpose[2].

The following quotations make the meaning more clear.

"Mankind was one community and Allah sent [unto them] prophets as bearers of good tidings and as warners, and revealed there with the Scripture with the Truth that it might judge between mankind concerning that wherein they differed, [None disputed it save those to whom it was given, after clear proofs had come unto them, through hatred one of another]. And Allah by His will guided those who believe unto the truth of that concerning which they differed. Allah guideth whom He will unto a straight path." 'Surah 2 Verse 213.

'These are the portents of Allah which We recite unto thee [Mohammad] with truth, and lo! Thou art of the number of [Our] messengers. Of these messengers, some of whom We have caused to excel others, and whom there are some unto whom Allah spoke, while some He exalted [above others] in degree; and We gave Jesus, son of Mary, clear proofs [of Allah's sovereignity and We supported him with the Holy Spirit And if Allah had so willed it, those who followed after him would not have fought one with another after the clear proof had come unto them. But they differed some of them believing and some disbelieving. But if Allah had so willed it, they would not have fought one with another, but Allah doeth what He will' Surah 2 verse 253.

'Lo! Those who believe [in that which is revealed unto thee Mohammad] and those who are Jews, and Christians and Sabaeen – who ever believeth in Allah and the Last day and doeth right — surely their reward is with their Lord and there shall no fear come upon them neither shall they grieve'. Surah 2 verse 48.

Surah 2 verse 135, 136 'They say, 'Accept the Jewish or the Christian faith and you shall be rightly guided.' Say: By no means! We believe in the faith of Abraham, the upright one. He was no idolator.'

'Nay but whosoever hath done evil and his sin surroundeth him, such are rightful owners of the Fire; they will abide therein.' Surah 2 verse 81

Surah 6 verse 161 Say: My Lord has guided me to a straight path, to an upright religion, to the faith of saintly Abraham, who was no idolator.'

Maulana Azad gives another proof of unity of all religions by pointing out that for 'good' the Quran uses the word 'Maroof' which means 'well known', and for 'bad' it uses 'munkar' which means 'that which has been forbidden'; This shows that according to Quran, both what is good and what is bad were known to humanity since earlier times because all religions and Divine books teach the same 'good acts' and forbid the same 'bad acts'.[3]

The Quran does not ask followers of other religions to forsake their own religion or Holy Book, writes Maulana Azad. The Quran tells them to follow their own religion in the proper way and also believe in the Quran as a Holy book and in prophet Mahammad as Allah's prophet, as Muslims have also been asked to believe in all prophets of Allah and in all Holy Books.

Time and again the Quran says that followers of all religions could have been following the same path if Allah so willed but they were given different codes by different prophets and each group thinks it is right and Allah will judge them on the day of Judgement. The concept of God in different religions was basically of One Supreme Being. This has been shown by research on religion and intensive studies undertaken by scholars to unearth the religious beliefs of ancient man. Maulana Azad writes that it has been found that the Indus Valley people believed in One God whom they called Oun. The concept of One God was also present in Hinduism or Sanathan Dharm, among the Greeks and the Iranians, as we have described earlier. The Quran also says so, as quoted earlier [Surah 2 verse 213] It was only later that people went astray and developed many differences among them selves regarding their religious beliefs. In most religions people started resorting to ancestor worship, worship of natural elements, Totemism, Manaism and Animism. Since it was difficult to concentrate on a Supreme Being without a form, people started worshipping idols whom they looked upon as representatives of the Supreme Being. Many also believed that these idols were the via media to establish a contact with Supreme Being. This was the belief of the Arabs too before the advent of the

Quran. Among the Semetic religions there was always the concept of One God and there was no idol worship, but after Christ, the Christians started the concept of Holy Trinity and Idol worship, which is against the teachings of the Holy Bible or Ingeel [Holy Book given to Jesus Christ.] The evolution in thought about the concept of Allah in the Semetic religions has been described very well by Maulana Azad. He writes that the Jews had a concept of a wrathful and overpowering God, who would punish wrong doers very harshly. Jesus tried to remove the fear from the minds of the people and propagated the concept of a loving and forgiving God who was like unto a father for the children. In all his teachings Jesus called himself the Son of Man as written in the various versions of the New Testament. He never said he was the Son of God. He likened God to a loving father to explain His love and care for humans. The Quran presents a very comprehensive concept of Allah, the Supreme Being. By the time the Quran was revealed human thought had developed to a great extent and man was able to think of a Supreme Being which was one of its own kind with no partner and with a unique presence which was not seen to others but which could see every one. The Quran also differentiated between the presence or entity of the Supreme Being and its attributes, which are all positive. Earlier religions had either personified the Supreme Being or created different gods for different attributes or powers. Hinduism talked of a Supreme Being which was Nirgun. Its philosophy stated that since the Supreme Being is not like any one else it is not possible to give it any attributes since all the attributes we know are of human nature. In the Semetic religions attributes were given to the Supreme Being, as mentioned above; the Jewish concept stressing the wrathfulness and avenging nature while Christian concept stressing the loving and forgiving nature. Islam presents ninety nine attributes of Allah which are known to human mind and all attributes are positive. Even when it is said that Allah is Jabbar and Qahhar it is understood that He is so to sinners who deserve punishment. Time and again the Quran says Allah is not cruel or unjust, He only punishes those who have done wrong as that is necessary for justice.

Islam is a universal religion in the sense that since the beginning of humanity, The Supreme Being has sent the same message to people through different prophets or messengers, saying that they should surrender their will to that of the Supreme Being whether you call Him Allah or God or Brahma or by any other name. All religions therefore teach obedience to The Supreme Being and faith in His powers. In Arabic the word for surrender to the Will of The Supreme Being is Islam. The Holy Quran says that right since the time of Adam Allah has sent the same message of Islam to the people. The Prophet Mohammad PBUH was the last prophet of Islam, who was given the last Holy book, Quran, to preach to the people and guide them on the right path. The Holy Quran is meant as a gift to the entire humanity and Allah says it is sent to guide all those who are interested in learning the truth and following the right path. The Prophet Mohammad too has been sent as a benevolent guide to the entire humanity. Muslims are expected to believe in all prophets and holy books, whether they are mentioned in the Quran or not, giving equal importance to all; hence it is only fair that followers of other religions too should believe that Mohamad PBUH is a prophet of God. The following Quranic quotations substantiate the above statement.

'Lo! We inspire thee as We inspired Noah and the prophets after him, as We inspired Abraham and Ismael and Isaac and Jacob and the tribes, and Jesus and Job and Jonah and Aaron and Solomon and as We imparted unto David the Psalms. And mesengers We have mentioned unto thee before and messengers We have not mentioned unto thee; and Allah spoke directly to Moses. Messengers of good cheer and of warning, in order that mankind might have no argument against Allah after the messengers; Allah was ever Mighty Wise'. Surah IV veres 163 - 165.

'Say my Lord enjoineth Justice, And set your faces upright [towards Him] at every place of worship and call upon Him [only] He brought you into being, so return ye unto'. [Him] Surah VII verse 29.

'Let the People of the Gospel judge by that which Allah hath revealed therein. Whoso judgeth not by that which Allah hath revealed such are evil livers. And unto thee have We revealed the Scripture with the Truth, confirming whatever Scripture was before it, and a watcher over it. So judge between them by that which Allah hath revealed and follow not their desires away from the Truth, which hath come unto thee. For each We have appointed a divine law and traced out a path. Had Allah willed He could have made you one community, but that He may try you by that which He hath given you [He hath made you as you are] So vie with one another in good works Unto Allah ye will all return and He will then inform you of that wherein ye differ'. Surah V verse 46-48.

'Revile not those unto whom they pray beside Allah lest they wrongfully revile Allah through ignorance Thus unto every nation have We made their deed seem fair Then unto their Lord is their return and He will tell them what they used to do.' Surah VI verse 108.

'Lo, Your religion is but one religion, and I am your only Lord. Therefore serve [worship] Me. Men have divided themselves into schisms, but to Us they shall all return.' Surah XX1 verse 92, 93.

The following quotations from the Quran show that Islam is the religion of all prophets, although it must have been known by different names in different times. The meaning of all religions has been surrender to a Supreme Being and in Arabic the word for it is Islam. In fact the Quran says prophet Abraham was a Muslim, prophet Joseph was a

Muslim, which shows that a Muslim is a believer in Supreme Being who surrenders his will to Him. In a broad sense, there could be Muslims in all faiths.

Surah 4 verse 125 'Who is better in religion than he who surrendereth his purpose to Allah while doing good [to men] and followeth the tradition of Abraham, the upright! Allah [Himself] chose Abraham for friend.'

Surah 16 verse 123 'And afterward We inspired thee [Mohammad, saying] Follow the religion of Abraham, as one by nature upright. He was not of the idolators.'

Surah 21 verses 48 – 50 "We showed Moses and Aaron the distinction between right and wrong, and gave them a light and admonition (Bible) for righteous men: those who truly fear their Lord and dread the terrors of Judgement day. And in this (Quran) We have revealed a blessed council. Will you then reject? We bestowed guidance and wisdom on Abraham according to his position, for We knew him well." "We gave him Isaac and then Jacob for a grandson; and We made each a righteous man. We ordained them leaders to guide mankind at Our behest, and enjoined on them good deeds [khairat], prayer [namaz] and almsgiving [zakat]" [verse 72-73]

Surah 22 verse 77 'Strive [jahadu] for the cause of Allah with the devotion due to Him. He has chosen you and laid on you no burdens in the observance of your faith, the faith of Abraham, your father. In this and in former scriptures, he has given you the name of Muslims, so that His apostle may testify against you may testify against your fellow men.'

Surah 12 verse 38 [Joseph said] 'I follow the faith of my forefathers, Abraham and Isaac and Jacob, It never was for us to attribute aught as partner to Allah. This is of the bounty of Allah unto us and unto mankind, Yet most men do not give thanks.'

Surah 12 verse 101 [Joseph prayed] 'Lord, You have given me power and taught me to interpret mysteries. You are the Creator of the heavens and the earth, my Guardian in this world and in the next. Let me die in submission [Muslim] and join the righteous.'

Surah 30 verse 30 'Therefore stand firm in your devotion to the true faith, which Allah Himself has made and for which he has made man. Allah's creation cannot be changed. This is surely the true religion, although most men do not know it.'

Many times the Quran tells the believers to believe in all prophets whom Allah sent from time to time and not to make any distinction among them, i.e. consider all equal in importance. The Quran also says that while some prophets have been named by Allah in the Quran many have not been named but believers should believe in all. Hence it is logical to assume that the Quran is not only addressing the Arabs but the entire humanity and asking it to believe in the eternal message of the Supreme Being, who is worshipped by all, in different ways and is called by different names. The following Quranic quotations explain this clearly.

Surah 4 verse 152: But those who believe in Allah and His messengers and make no distinction between any of them Allah will give their wages and Allah was ever Forgiving, Merciful.

Surah 5 verse 3 [Allah says] This day have I perfected your religion for you and completed My favour unto you and have chosen for you as religion AL ISLAM.

Later on in this Surah Allah says how He had taken an oath from the Jews and the Christians that they will obey Him and believe in His messengers and support them, but except a few, they forgot the covenant. Then Allah tells them about prophet Mohammad as follows:

> Surah 5 verse 15: People of the Book! Our apostle has come to reveal to you much of what you have hidden of

the Scriptures, and to forgive you much. A light has come to you from Allah and a glorious Book with which He will guide to the paths of peace those that seek to please Him; He will lead them by His will from darkness to the light; He will guide them to a straight path.

Here it behoves us to understand clearly that while the religion or Deen has been the same for all humanity, the Sharia or code of conduct and customs and traditions for different peoples have been different due to changed times and changed circumstances. Maulana Azad has explained this beautifully in his Tarjumanul Quran. In Surah 5, i.e., Maida, Allah tells Prophet Mohammad that the Torah was given to the Jews as a guide and their prophets and later on their Rabbis and religious leaders had followed its injunctions and settled their disputes according to its teachings. Allah tells the Jews to also do the same and follow the teachings of Torah and not change its contents or meaning. After Torah, Jesus was given Injeel which was also a light and guidance for his people. It also confirmed the Torah. The followers of Jesus are asked to follow the teachings of the Injeel [Gospel] and settle their disputes according to it. In the end Prophet Mohammad has been given the Quran which again is a light and guidance for all. It confirms the Gospel and Torah and is also a watcher over them, because people had tampered with the teachings of earlier scriptures and Allah has promised to safe guard the Quran Himself. The Quran has been revealed to preserve the truth that was revealed in earlier scriptures and it also preserves the basic purpose of religion which was the same in all divine revelations. Later on Allah tells in the same Surah as follows:

Surah 5 verse 66 If the People of the Book accept the true faith and keep from evil, We will pardon them their sins and admit them to the gardens of delight. If they observe the Torah and the Gospel and what is revealed to them from Allah, they shall be given abundance from above and from beneath. Some of them are righteous men but many of them do nothing but evil.

This shows all those who will follow their own divine book properly and have faith in the Supreme Being and all His apostles and Books and do good will be rewarded.

The following quotations show that prophets were sent from time to time to different peoples, by Allah with the same message.

Surah 14 verse 9 - 12 Have you not heard what befell the nations that have gone before you? The people of Noah, Aad and Thamoud, and those who came after? Allah alone knows their number. Their apostles came to them with veritable signs, but they shut their mouths with their hands and said:' we will not believe in your message. Indeed we strongly doubt the faith to which you call us.' Their apostles answered: 'Is there any doubt about Allah, the Creator of the heavens and the earth? He calls you to Him that He may forgive you your sins and respite you till your appointed hour.'

Surah 10 verse 19 'Mankind were but one community then they differed; and had it not been for a word that had already gone forth from thy Lord, it had been Judged between them in respect of that wherein they differ.'

Surah 6 verse 161 Say Lo! As for me, my Lord hath guided me unto a straight path, a right religion, the community of Abraham, the upright, who was no idolator. [quoted earlier too].

Surah 7 verse 29 Say my Lord enjoineth Justice And set your faces upright [towards Him] at every place of worship and call upon Him, making religion pure for Him [alone] As He brought you into being, so return ye[unto Him].

Surah 7 verse 35 'O children of Adam ! when messengers of your own come unto you who narrate unto you My revelations, then whosoever refraineth from evil and amendeth, then shall no fear come upon them neither shall they grieve.'

Surah 16 verses 120 - 123 Lo! Abraham was the spiritual head of a nation obedient to Allah, by nature upright, and he was not of the idolators. Thankful for His bounties; so He chose him and guided him unto a straight path. And We gave him good in this world and in the Hereafter he is among the righteous. And afterward We inspired thee [Mohammad, saying] Follow the religion of Abraham, as one by nature upright. He was not of the idolators.

Surah 42 verse 13 He has ordained for men the faith He has revealed to you [Mohammad] and formerly enjoined on Noah and Abraham, on Moses and Jesus, saying : Observe this faith and be united in it. But that to which you call them is unacceptable to the idolators Allah chooses for it whom He will, and guides to it those that repent.

Surah 42 verse 15 Therefore call men to the true Faith, and follow the straight path as you are bidden.

The Quran clarifies that all messengers spoke of One God and all those who follow their religion correctly will be rewarded by Him. It is also mentioned that all religions should co-exist and people should worship the Lord as they have been taught by their apostles. The Quran is the final message of the Supreme Being for people of all religions and tells them to follow their own religions in the pure form as taught by the apostles and give up all incorrect beliefs and customs that have crept into their religious traditions. The following quotation proves this.

Surah 5 verse 7 "This day I have perfected your religion for you and completed my favour to you. I have chosen Islam to be your faith."

The enlightened men have also been doing, the same, i.e., try to remove incorrect beliefs and practices from various religious faiths, from time to time, both in our country and in other parts of the world, because man has been endowed with spiritual wisdom and he can realize it if he makes an effort in the right direction. In our country, Guru Nanak tried to combine the teachings of Hinduism and Islam and present a new religion, Sikhism. The Sufi saints like Khwaja Moinuddin Chishti, Sabir Pir and Baba Farid tried to unite people of all faiths by their teachings. The poet Kabir too worked towards uniting people of different faiths. While some of his Dohas are based on Bhagwad Gita, some others are based on Quran. Hindus like Swamy Vivekananda and Raja Ram Mohan Roy tried to purify the Hindu religion by removing the post-Vedic accretions, in the 19th and 20th centuries. During the British rule when Christian missionaries pointed out the unjust treatment of low castes and women in Hinduism, the enlightened Hindus realized that these evil practices should be given up. So they referred to Vedas and Upnishads to prove that these practices were not prevalent in Vedic period and were in fact post Vedic accretions. They worked hard to convince people to give up practices like Sati and Untouchablity Similarly Sir Syed Ahmad Khan had to convince the Muslims that acquiring modern English education is not un Islamic. He had to face a lot of opposition before he could succeed in spreading modern education among Muslims. He did not promote women's education, though. Probably he thought the time was not ripe for it. Later Sheikh Abdullah promoted education for girls at Aligarh with the help of his wife. From time to time reformers have tried to bring about positive changes in their communities, by interpreting their respective religions in a liberal way, in different parts of the world, but the final divine message for the whole world, to give up wrong practices and surrender their will to the Supreme Being as taught by their prophets, is the Quran. Therefore the Quran enjoins all humanity to believe in the Quran as the final message from the Almighty and in Mohammad[pbuh] as the final messenger of the Almighty.

The following quotations explain it better.

Surah 21 verse 25 We inspired all the apostles whom We sent before you, saying : There is no god but Me. Therefore serve Me.

Surah 5 verse 47: For each We have appointed a divine law and a traced out way. Had Allah willed He could have made you one community. But that He may try you by that which He hath given you[He hath made you as you are] so vie one with another in good works Unto Allah ye will all return, and He will then inform you of that wherein ye differ

Surah 14 Verse 4: Each apostle We have sent has spoken only in the language of his own people, so that he might make plain to them his message

Surah 22 verse 34-35 For every nation We have ordained a ritual, that they may pronounce the name of Allah over the beasts which He has given them for food. Your God is one God; to Him surrender yourselves. Give good news to the humble, whose hearts are filled with awe at the mention of their Lord; who endure their misfortunes with fortitude, attend to their prayers and bestow in charity of that which We have given them.

Surah 22 verse 67 "For every nation We have ordained a ritual which they observe. Let them not dispute with you concerning this. Call them to the path of your Lord: you are rightly guided."

The above quotations make clear that different nations have their own rules and traditions for doing things which were taught to them by their prophets, so they should follow them but basically their faith and their notion of good and bad should be the same. Quran is not nullifying the earlier traditions but presenting God's message in the true form once again, because many wrong notions had been adopted by followers of earlier apostles; and also giving the rituals and Shariat for the followers of prophet Mohammad. The message brought by him is meant for the entire humanity.

The following quotations make it clear that prophet Mohammad has been sent for the entire humanity:

> Surah 4 verse 170 'O mankind the messenger hath come unto you with the Truth from your Lord; Therefore believe.'

Surah 7 verse 158 'Say to your people I am sent forth to you by Allah His is the Kingdom of the heavens and the earth. There is no God but Him He ordains life and death. Therefore have faith in Allah and His apostle, the Unlettered Prophet, who believes in Allah and His word. Follow him so that you may be rightly guided.'

Surah 21 verse106 'We sent thee[Mohammad] not save as a mercy for all mankind.'

Surah 33 verse 40 'He [Mohammad] is the apostle of Allah and the Seal of the Prophets.'

Surah 48 verse 28 - 29 'It is He [Allah] that has sent forth His apostle with guidance and the true faith, so that he may exalt it above all religions, Allah is the all sufficient Witness. Mohammad is Allah's apostle.'

While Prophet Mohammad is told again and again in the Quran about earlier prophets and their noble deeds and ordered to follow in their footsteps the Quran also tells us that earlier prophets had prophesied about the coming of Mohammad [pbuh] just as prophets before Jesus had prophesied about his coming. The following quotation shows how Jesus spoke of the coming of Mohammad.

Surah 61verses 6-8 And when Jesus son of Mary said, 'O children of Israel ! Lo! I am the messenger of Allah unto you, confirming that which was [revealed] before me in the Torah and bringing good tidings of a messenger who cometh after me, whose name is the Praised one[Ahmad]. Yet when he hath come unto them with clear proofs, they say,'This is more magic'.

Surah 7 verse 157 [Allah told Moses] I will show mercy to those that keep from evil, give alms and believe in Our signs: and to those that shall follow the Apostle – the unlettered Prophet- whom they shall find described in the Torah and the Gospel. He will enjoin righteousness upon them and forbid them from evil. He will make good things lawful to them and prohibit all that is foul. He will relieve them of their burdens and of the shakles that weigh upon them. Those that believe in him and honour him, those that aid him and follow the light to be sent forth with him, shall surely triumph.' At another place in the Quran it is said Prophet Abraham prayed to Allah in Mecca to send a prophet from among the Meccans to preach the Word of God to them and in answer to this prayer Allah sent prophet Mohammad. Abraham's prayer is as follows:

> Surah 2 Verse 129. Lord send forth to them an apostle of their own who shall declare to them Your Revelations and instruct them in the Scriptures and in wisdom and purify them of sin.

There are many verses in the Quran which tell us about the earlier prophets, their tribulations and their steadfastness. This is one way of providing solace to prophet Mohammad and asking him not to grieve if he is persecuted, disbelieved and reviled. It also shows that all apostles were sent by the same God to spread His message and to warn wrong doers. It has been God's custom to send messengers to each nation.

Surah 13 verses 38, 39 'We did send messengers before thee, and appointed for them wives and children, and it was never the part of a messenger to bring a Sign, except as Allah permitted. For each period is an appointment. Allah doth blot out or confirm what He pleaseth, With Him is the Mother of the Book.' This quotation gives solace to Prophet Mohammad and also clarifies that Allah sends what Message or Sign He likes to different people through different prophets but the Main Book or the Eternal Truth is safe with Him.

Surah 17 verse 15 'Nor do We punish a nation until We have sent forth an apostle to warn them.' This shows that apostles were sent to all communities of the world. Those who did not believe were punished.

Surah 35 verse 22- 25 'We have sent you with the truth to proclaim good news and to warn your people; for there is no nation that has not been warned by an apostle. If they disbelieve you, know that those who have gone before them also disbelieved. Their apostles came to them with veritable signs, with scriptures and with the light giving Book.

Surah 40 verse 78 'We did aforetime send messengers before thee: of them there are some whose story We have related to thee and some whose story We have not related to thee; it was not [possible] for any Messenger to bring a Sign except by the leave of Allah. But when the command of Allah issued, the matter was decided in truth and justice, and there perished, there and then, those who stood on falsehoods.'

Surah 43 verse 6 'Many a prophet did We send forth to the ancients: but they scoffed at each prophet that arose amongst them. We utterly destroyed them, though they were mightier than these.' These two quotes are meant to pacify Prophet Mohammad whom the non believers always asked for miracles and taunted him by saying that if he is true then he should bring retribution on them at once.

Some more quotations about the universal message sent through the Holy Quran are as follows:

Surah 42 verse 13 'He has ordained for men the faith He has revealed to you and formerly enjoined on Noah and Abraham, on Moses and Jesus, saying : Observe this Faith and be united in it.'

Surah 45 verse 20 'This [Quran] is clear indication for mankind and a guidance and a mercy for a folk whose faith is sure.'

Surah 46 verse 12 'Yet before it [Quran] the Book of Moses was revealed, a guide and a blessing to all men. This Book confirms it. It is revealed in the Arabic tongue to forewarn the wrong doers and to give good news to the righteous.'

The Quran says that if someone is attacked for following their religion Allah allows them to retaliate and will help them, be it any religion. The following quotation makes this clear.

Surah 22 verse 39- 41 'Permission to take up arms is hereby is given to those who are attacked, because they have been wronged. Allah has power to grant them victory: those who have been unjustly driven from their homes only because they said: Our Lord is Allah.' Had Allah not checked [repelled] some men by the might of others, the monasteries and churches, the synagogues and the mosques in which His praise is daily celebrated, would have been utterly destroyed. But whosoever helps Allah shall be helped by Him. Allah is powerful and mighty: He will assuredly help those who once made masters in the land, will attend to their prayers and pay the alms-tax, enjoin justice and forbid evil. Allah controls the destiny of all things.'

This last quotation makes it very clear that Allah will help all those who are conscious of their duty to their creator and their fellow beings, be they the followers of any apostle, because basically all worship one Supreme Being, be it in a mosque, in a church or in a synagogue.

Its not as if the authors have come up with some new or revolutionary idea by saying that all religions preach the same message of surrendering one's will to a Supreme Being and trying to do good and avoid evil. Great thinkers and intellectuals as well as religious leaders in all ages have expressed similar views from time to time. On the other hand there are some thinkers who are of the opinion that while Judaism, Christianity and Islam are monotheistic religions with a lot in common, older religions like Hinduism Buddhism and Jainism are different and not monotheistic.

To subtantiate the former school of thought, many quotations from the writings of scholars of different faiths are being given here. Baba Virsa Singh writes an article entitled, 'Messages of All Prophets Come From One Source, in which he says, God chooses prophets and when the right time comes, gives them gyan or knowledge. The chosen ones become receivers of divine revelations. After God begins using a person as His Mesenger, that person no longer works from his own mind or his own heart. It is all God's work. All prophets have come from the same light; they all give the same basic messages. None have come to change the older revealed scriptures; they have come to remind people of the earlier prophets' messages which the people have forgotten. We have made our separate religions into fortresses, each claiming one of the prophets as its own, but the Light of God cannot be confined to manmade structures. It radiates throughout all Creation. No prophet belongs to just one caste, creed or nation. Jesus is not confined to Christianity, Moses is not only a Jew, Prophet Mohammad is not only a Muslim and Guru Nanak is not only a Sikh. They have not come to establish institutionalised, sectarian religions. Prophets come into the world with a message from God. They come to remind people of divine teachings, making them fresh and new again. They enlighten people and show them how to live. As human beings we do have spiritual wisdom deep within us; the One who creates the world is already within us. But it is only when a prophet comes and starts speaking with divine wisdom, that it awakens this knowledge within us. [Times of India 5-1-08][5]

Devendra Uppal writes an article 'Why the Rig Veda is Common Heritage' 'to explain the universal appeal of the Rig Veda. He writes that the truth revealed by the Vedas is universal. In the Vedas God is said to be the One who never leaves us, in life, death or otherwise. God is Truth,

Knowledge, Infinite and Ultimate : i.e. Satyam, Gyanam, Anantam and Brahm. The only One is balancing the planets and controlling the cosmos continuously. His name is the greatest and most potent of all. A Vedic hymn says, 'You [God] are never away from us but strange it is that we cannot see you'. God belongs to the innocent and the pure and protects them too. God revealed himself to sages in their meditation and they penned down Truth about Him and the universe. [Times of India, Oct. 2007][6], In Common Ideals in Vedanṭa and Sufi Philosophy, Pranav Khullar, writes about how the Mughal Prince, Dara Shikoh would spend long hours striving to undertand a consciousness which dreamt of universal brotherhood. Dara Shikoh's spiritual longing and quest for reality or Haquiqat and Unity or Tawheed led him to study the Upanihads, 52 of which he translated from Sankrit to Persian, in his Sirr-e Akbar [The Great Secret] Focussing attention on the 'treasure of Monotheim' found in the Upanihads, Dara Shikoh draws remarkable parallels between concepts elucidated in the Holy Quran and the Upanishads with respect to Tawheed. His Sufi state of mind even assigned the status of Kitab-I-Maknun, well protected book, to the Upanishads, convinced that the Quran and the Upanishads represented two different facets of that One Self. Dara's attempt to draw these similarities between Vedantic traditions and the ideas embodied in the Quran may have cost him his life but his exploration was a pioneering effort at religious syncretism. A search for a common thread between Vedanta and Sufi thought led him into elaborate discourse on cosmogony in his Majma ul Bahrayn – Mingling of two Oceans- as conceptualised in Hinduism and Islam. He tried to show the similarity between the Hindu Panchbhutas and five great elements of Islamic thought. Similarly the five senses mentioned in Islamic thought correspond to the panch indriyas of Hindu philosophy. Drawing on his personal experience with Sufis and yogis, Dara Shikoh strove to underline the common vision of two great traditions, through his passionate analyis of similar mystic language and concepts[7]. A A R Crollius writes in greater detail about Dara Shikoh's Majma al Bahrayn in an article in the book, Islam in India. He writes that the direction Dara Shikoh took in his search for the truth, not beyond religious creeds and systems, but precisely in the meeting of their most inner being at the Source of all truth and life, is very important and relevant to this day. A meeting of religions is made possible not by 'transcending' their particularities. Rather it is by humbly investigating and sharing what the respective religious creeds and ways of life contain as their most precious and noble aspirations that the way to a possible convergence becomes manifest. Dara Shikoh writes that having collected the views of the two parties, i.e. Sufi and Indian monotheists and having brought together the points– a knowledge of which is absolutely essential and useful for the seekers of Truth- he has compiled a tract and entitled it Majma al bahrayn or The Mingling of the two Oceans, as it is a collection of the truth and wisdom of two Truth-knowing [haqq shinas] groups. Discussing the title, Crollius writes Majma al bahrayn is of Quranic origin and has been mentioned in several places. It has been said in the Quran that the two meet [but] they do not encroach upon each other [55: 19] meaning that the characteristics of the two remain distinct. In accordance with this representation we would prefer to translate majma as meeting and not mingling. Dara Shikoh's premature death prevented him from elaborating on his notes, but perhaps at a time when religious pluralism does no longer imply communal antagonism, and when those who seek the truth, desire to share it rather than to defend it, the meeting to which the Majma al bahrayn is a prelude can finally come about, whilst still maintaining the distinctive character of each group involved.[8]

Prof. Habib, the noted historian, has written about relation between Muslims and non Muslims in the introduction he has written to the book, Khilafat to Partition by Moin Shakir. He quotes many Muslim thinkers and saints to show that they all were of the opinion that God has created all men and they have to coexist and follow their own traditions. He writes, 'Muslim mystics of the highest grade have had no hesitation in answering the question of the relation of Muslims and non Muslims. Shaikh Mohiuddin ibn i Arabi, the greatest thinker Islam has produced, declared that the difference between Islam and 'shirk' is phenomenal not real, for both are the integral and necessary parts of a Divinely ordered universe. Maulana Rumi drove this lesson home in his Masnawi by many verses of the highest order. In some lines composed as a message from Allah to Moses the Masnawi says: To every people We have granted a basis of virtue [sirat]; to every people We have granted a religious technique [istilah]. The religious technique of Sindh is best for the Sindhis [Muslims] and the religious technique of India is best for the Hindus. To the vulgar question as to what would happen in the next world to non Muslims of excellent character who believe in God- Shaikh Nizamuddin Aulia replied emphatically 'This is a matter for God to decide in His mercy; you cannot decide the matter for Him.' Shaikh Naseeruddin Chiragh of Delhi asked his biographer to remember that in the famous Quranic verse,'and as to those who strive for Us We will lead them to Our paths [subulana]' the word paths was in the plural not singular [sabilana]. There are many paths to God; whatever fanatics, in their ignorance, may assert, Islam did not come to close the gates of Divine mercy on mankind.[9]

While there is much that is common between Quran and Bible and Gospel, there are many similarities among all other religious scriptures too. Research has shown that there are similarities between the contents of two ancient scriptures, namely the Vedas and the Zend Avesta. There are many similarities between teachings of Vedas and the Quran to the extent that same words [in different languages] have been used, to describe the attributes of the

Almighty, as shown by many scholars. The three types of human self which are found among men, have been described as Nafs e Ammara [baser self] Nafs e Lawwama [self which repents] Nafs e Mutmainna [self which is highly satisfied with respect to his Creator] in the Quran; in the Gita there are three corresponding names for the same; namely Tamasa [mode of ignorance], Rajasah [mode of pasion] and Sattvika [mode of goodness] [Chapter 17 Text 4 Bhagvad Gita]. While Quran tells humanity again and again to surrender to the Almighty the Bhagavad Gita also tells the same; "O scion of Bharata, surrender unto Him utterly. By His grace you will attain transcendental peace and supreme and eternal abode." [Chapter 18 Text 62] Similarly while the Quran says "Say Allah is One, the Self Sufficient God. He begot none nor was He begotten. None is equal to Him." [Surah 112 verses 1-4] the Gita says "He who knows Me as the unborn, as the beginning less, as the Supreme Lord of all the worlds – he, undeluded among men, is freed from all sin." [Chapter 10 Text 3] Another similarity in the content of the two scriptures is as follows: The Quran says, "Each day of His is like a thousand years in your reckoning." [Surah 22 verse 47] and the Gita says, "By human calculation, a thousand ages taken together is the duration of Brahma's one day: and such also is the duration of His night." [Chapter 8 Text 17]

Many scholars have also written about the differences among various religions, specially between the monotheistic and poly theistic religions. Here I would like to quote from the work of the emminent sociologist Prof. Yogendra Singh. In his book Modernization of the Indian Tradition, he writes about Hinduism as follows: Theoretically the Veda represent the Revelation of Hinduism and all its cultural patterns. But in practice from time to time new innovations and additions were always made in the structure of this tradition. Hinduism is not a religious system alone but represents a way of life. It constitutes a distinctive world view and a cultural complex. The principles of hierarchy, holism and continuity are abstracted from the view point of 'order' one of the two characteristics of Hindu Great Tradition. From the view point of the other characteritic, 'change' we get the cyclical devolutionary conception. The normative principles of Hinduism have been as meticulouly systematic and closed as its empirical structure has been varied and amorphous. Behind the extreme degree of permissiveness and liberalism in beliefs and variety in ritual practices as admitted by Hindu cannonical system, there exists a strictly logical view of phenomena in terms of which principles of 'order' and 'change', 'being' and 'becoming' and 'creation' and 'destruction' and so on can be meaningfully explained.

In contradistinction to the structure of the Hindu Great Tradition, the Great Tradition of Islam is founded on a world view which is apparently non-hierarchical, is purely monotheistic and messianic-historical in ethos. Emphasis on the historical nature of the tradition is paramount in all Abrahamanic religions but in Islam it is most prominent. This emphasis on the historicity of the revealed tradition has rendered the world view of Islam not only more proselytizing or activistic in the sphere of religion but also makes it holistic and socio centric in general cultural orientation. Islam does not admit of any institutionalised role for priests; the 'ulema' are in no sense the priests, rather they correspond to the 'scribes' in Judaism. Strictly speaking Islam has no 'clergy' as any Muslim may lead a congregation in prayer. Islam has a more developed orientation towards holistic principle in its conception of social order than Hinduism. In Hinduism the principle of holism is a coordinate of the principle of hierarchy; in the revealed tradition of Islam the principle of holism is sociologically, though not in principle, differentiated from hierarchism, as there is less substansive place for the latter in the tradition. The typical nature of this holism and the emphasis on the historicity of the tradition have introduced elements of insularity and exclusiveness in Islam. Islamic holism is based on the unity of the Muslim 'umma', the collectivity of the faithful and 'millat' the one nation of believers [cutting across geographic boundaries] This holistic principle has, unlike in the Hindu tradition, a radical egalitarian connotation, though the elements of equality as existent in Islamic tradition are logically foreclosed [and are not open ended as in the modern world view] within the framework of the tradition. Equality is thus meaningful within the immutable and the sacerdotal contexts of the principles of holism and hierarchy. On this level there is a transcendent unity not only between Hinduism and Islam but amongst all sacred traditions.

Writing about Muslim rule in India, Yogendra Singh discusses the various attempts made at religious syncretism by the Muslim rulers, Sufi saints Muslim poets and literary figures. Non-ritualism and abstract monotheism as preached by Sufi saints was not only appealing to the Hindu masses but also tended to be in harmony with their forces of introversion and retreatism that had overtaken Hindu tradition after its loss of political power.'But he concludes that there continues to be a politico cultural insularity between the two great traditions in India, inspite of cultural syncretism because there was never a mutual cultural acceptance.[10] Here I would like to note some important points made by Singh which are favourable to my thesis of religious unity: He says Hindu religion also has 'revealed tradition' in the form of Vedas. He says although the empirical structure of Hinduism is amorphous, the normative principles are meticulously systematic and closed [as in Islamic shariat] Finally he does point out some similarities in both religions. Secondly it is important to note some comments he makes about Islam, which are generally not known to people: He says there is no institutionalized role for priests in Islam, in fact there is no 'clergy' in Islam. Very few people know this or would believe this because the Mullahs have a stranglehold on the common Muslims, specially in India. So much so that a learned person like Mr Arun Shourie said in a Television discussion that Islam is a religion which is based on a text which is difficult to understand and can be explained only by the clergy. It was surprising that two Muslims on the panel did not refute him. The truth is that any one who wants to understand the Quran can start reading it with real concentration and hope for guidance and surely God will guide him. In Surah 54 Allah has repeated again and again the following verse; "We have made the Quran easy to understand : but will any take heed?" Those verses which are Mohakamat [clear orders and instructions] should be followed and those which are Mutashabihat {not clear in meaning} should be believed in as Word of God. Constant diligence may reward the reader with new and more profound understanding. Allah has said in the Quran that He alone shows the right path to those who seek it. The Gospel says some thing similar,' Seek and it shall be opened unto you'. The Bhagwad Gita too gives many similar messages, like "He who meditates on the Supreme Personality of Godhead, his mind constantly engaged in remembering Me, undeviated from the path, he O Partha, is sure to reach Me." [Chapter 8 Text 8] and "To those who are contantly devoted and worship Me with love, I give the understanding by which they can come to Me." [Chapter 10 Text 10] and also "For one who remembers Me without deviation I am easy to obtain, O son of Partha, because of his constant engagement in devotional service." [Chapter 8 Text 14][11].

There are various other writers and thinkers who have tried to show the unity of all religions, and have quoted extensively from different scriptures to show similarity of content. In this connection the following quotation from an article written by Marguerite Theophil, an organisational consultant in Mumbai, seems relevant; 'While each Tradition has teachings from its own followers, many of these teachings, while rooted in this or that faith, are also gifts to those from other faiths/traditions. All it needs is a respectful openness of spirit; truth comes to us in many forms.'[12] Efforts are on in the West and in Iran to stress the common origin of the three monotheistic religions and to put an end to hatred and ill will among their followers. In India, Zakir Naik has done a lot of research to show similarities between Vedas and the Quran and through Peace TV he is trying to spread the message of unity of religion.

Dr. Rafiq Zakaria, in his masterly work on the evolution of human thought regarding the Supreme Being, entitled 'Discovery of God', writes in one place, 'The search for one God began in a hesitant but some what organised way about two thousand years ago, initially in Meso potania. Its traces were no doubt visible in Egypt, India, China and Iran, Greece and Italy took to the creed rather later. There after the Arabian peninsula saw its full flowering. In most of these countries relies have been found to confirm the trend. The earliest man known to recorded history, who was able to give monolithic aspirations to the spiritual urge was Hammurabi. He ruled over the Kingdom of Babylon. He proclaimed with all the power and Majesty at his command that hence forth idols and icons would no longer be worshipped; in then place only one God, Marduk, who symbolised justice and fair play for all, would be revealed.'[13]

In conclusion the author would like to present her own views on the unity of all religions. The Quran declares that Islam is not a new religion but the universal religion which was preached by different prophets at different times and in different places. Naturally the earlier prophets must have been given scriptures suitable to the level of intelligence of their people and they must have interpreted them in their own way. In later periods religion was presented in more compact, comprehensive and crystallised form and the entire message was preserved in the form of Holy Books. The Vedas are the ancient scriptures and research has found many similarities in the content of Vedas and the Quran. It is quite logical and sensible to assume that there must have been apostles of God among the ancient Rishis of India and learned people in Iran, Greece and other places. They all must have been given the knowledge of the eternal truth by God which they taught to their people. Sri Ram and Sri Krishna also must have been apostles of God and Bhagvad Gita was given to Sri Krishna. Over the centuries people must have started considering them as avtars rather than apostles of God. Buddha, Mahavira, Confucious and Zoroaster must have also been apostles of God who brought the same message from Him. With the passage of time many wrong notions enter the religious traditions. Although Islam is the most recent of world religions, accretions have been made in its tradition too. A common fault of humanbeings has been to deify saints and apostles The Quran says about this as follows: 'To Allah alone is true worship due. As for those who choose other guardians beside Him, saying: 'We serve them only that they may bring us nearer to Allah,' Allah Himself will judge for them their differences. He does not guide the untruthful disbeliever.' [Surah 39 verse 3]

Thus we see that while some changes have occurred in the traditions of all religions with passage of time, it is quite logical to believe that all religions originated from the same source hence are the same and teach the same basic principles of leading a good life. It is wrong to fight in the name of religion or try to run down any religion. All religions were sent by the same Supreme Being and profess the universal truth.

TRANSLATIONS: N J Dawood [1978] The Quran A Tranlation Allen Lane London.

Mohd. M Pickthall Holy Quran English Translation.

References

1. GS Bhatt 2003, Sociology of Religion Unit 19 Hinduism IGNOU Publication.
2. Maulana Abul Kalam Azad Tarjumanul Quran.

3. Maulana Azad. ”
4. Maulana Azad. ”
5. Singh Virsa Times of India 5.1.08 the Speaking Tree.
6. Uppal Times of India Oct. 2007 the Speaking Tree.
7. Khullar Times of India 5.11.2008 the Speaking Tree.
8. Troll WC [1982] Islam in India Vikas Publishing.
9. Moin Shakir [1970] Khilafat to Partition Kalamkar Publication.
10. Singh Yogendra [1973] Modernization of the Indian Tradition, Manohar.
11. AC Bhaktivedanta Bhagvad Gita As It Is Collier Macmillan Publishers Swamy Prabhupada 1972.
12. Times of India 16th June 2008.
13. Zakaria Rafiq [2000] Discovery of God. Popular Prakashan.

3

The Relevance of Islam in Modern Times

Islam, as explained in the previous chapter is actually a universal religion, which has been taught from time to time by different messengers of the Supreme Being, to their people. The message was always the same as it was sent by the same Supreme Being whom people of different times worshipped by different names. Even today the teachings of the univeral religion are relevant for the modern man, as more and more learned men are realising and preaching in their discourses on art of living and achieving contentment. The teachings of the Vedas, the lessons taught in the Gita, the Ten Commandments, the Sermon on the Mount and the Last Khutba [discourse] of the Prophet Mohammad are all full of sound advice to lead a successful and purposeful life, hence they are useful for all times. Some variations in conditions and usages are natural, but the basic principles remain the same. In this chapter we will try to present quotations from the Quran to show how the Quran has given advice on common, day to day dealings and problems and suggestions and injunctions to solve the problems and maintain the best of relations with fellow human beings. There are instructions about treatment of relatives and other fellow beings, about using money properly, about being just in all activities, about carrying on trade and business, about property rights, about good manners and ettiquette. There are also verses that provide comfort and solace to men thus reducing tension. There are verses which show what is forbidden and should be avoided. There are verses which discuss common social evils. All these quotations exhibit the relevance of Quran for all times and for all mankind. The Quran clarifies what are the good acts which will make life better and what are the bad or wrong acts which should be avoided. We will now present Quranic quotations about various aspects of daily life which are relevent in modern times not from a religious point of view but from a secular point of view as they apply to reason and are based on sound common sense.

SOCIAL RELATIONS Quotations about treatment of fellowbeings and proper social behaviour are being given below.

Surah 4 verse 36, "Serve Allah and associate none with Him. Show kindness to your parents and your kindred, to the orphans and the needy, to your near and distant neighbours, to your fellow travellers, to the way farers and to the slaves whom you own."

Surah 4 verse 19 "Treat them[wives] with kindness; for even if you do not love them, it may well be that you may dislike a thing which Allah has meant for your own good" Surah 4 verse 58 "Allah commands you to hand back your trusts to their rightful owners, and to pass judgement upon men with fairness. Noble is that to which Allah exhorts you. He hears all and observes all'

Surah 6 verses 152 –154 "Do not tamper with the property of the orphans, but strive to improve their lot until they reach maturity. Give just weight and full measure; We never charge a soul with more than it can bear. Speak for justice, even if it affects your own kinsmen. Be true to the covenant of Allah. Thus Allah exhorts you, so that you may take heed."

Surah 7 verse 199, 200 "Show forgiveness, instruct about good deeds and avoid the ignorant. If Satan tempts you, seek refuge in Allah; He hears all and knows all. If those that guard themselves against evil are tempted by Satan, they have but to recall Allah's precepts and they shall see the light."

Surah 16 verse 91 92 "Keep faith with Allah when you make a covenant with Him. Do not break your oaths after you have sworn them: for by swearing in His name you make Allah your surety. Allah has knowledge of all your actions."

Surah 13 verse 20- 24 'Truly, none will take heed but the wise: those who keep faith with Allah and do not break their pledge; who join together what He has bidden to be united; who fear their Lord and dread the terrors of Judgement –day; who for the sake of Allah endure with fortitude, attend to their prayers, and give alms in private and in public, and who ward off evil with good. These shall have a blissful end.'

Surah 16 verse 126 "If you punish let your punishment be proportionate to the wrong that has been done to you. But it shall be best for you to endure your wrongs with .patience. Be patient then; Allah will grant you patience."

Surah 17 verse 23 – 25 "Your Lord has enjoined you to worship none but Him, and to show kindness to your parents. If either or both of them attain old age in your dwelling, show them no sign of impatience, nor rebuke them;but speak to them kind words. Treat them with humility and tenderness and say:' Lord be merciful to them, as they nursed me when I was an infant."

Surah 22 verse 41 "Allah is powerful and mighty: He will assuredly help those who, once made masters in the land, will attend to their prayers and pay the alms tax, enjoin justice and forbid evil. Allah controls the destiny of all things."

Surah 31 verses 17 – 19 [Luqman said] "My son, be steadfast in prayer, enjoin justice and forbid evil. Endure with fortitude whatever befalls you. That is a duty encumbent on all. Do not treat men with scorn, nor walk proudly on the earth: Allah does not love the arrogant and the vainglorious. Rather let your gait be modest and your voice low: the harshest of voices is the braying of the ass."

Surah 41 verse 34 – 36 "Good and evil deeds are not alike. Requite evil with good, and he who is your enemy will become your dearest friend. But none will attain this save those who endure with fortitude and are greatly favoured by Allah. If Satan tempts you, seek refuge in Allah. He hears all and knows all"

Surah 15 verse 85 "It was to reveal the truth that We created the heavens and the earth and all that lies between them. The Hour of Doom is sure to come:therefore forgive them [unbelievers] nobly."

Surah 42 verses 37 – 44 Let evil be rewarded with evil. But he that forgives and seeks reconciliation shall be rewarded by Allah. He does not love the wrong doers. Those who avenge themselves when wronged incur no guilt. But great is the guilt of those who oppress their fellowmen and conduct themselves with wickedness and injustice. These shall be sternly punished. To endure with fortitude and to forgive is a duty incombent on all. He whom Allah leads astray has none to protect him."

Surah 61 verses 2-3 'Believers, why do you profess what you never do? It is most odious in Allah's sight that you should say one thing and do another.'

There are many more similar quotations but the above mentioned more or less cover all important aspects of good behaviour towards fellowbeings. It is to be noted that while talking of orphans, widows, neighbours and travellers, there is no mention of their religion or faith, which means one should be kind to all irrespective of their faith. Similarly one has to be just to all even if it is against your own dear one. The instructions regarding revenge and forgiveness also apply to all and one has to appreciate the importance given to practical reality and human nature. Man would like to avenge, naturally; so he has been allowed to do so with out feeling guilty but if he forgives and leaves the matter to God he would be showing his better nature and would be rewarded for it. Some common shortcomings of people, like saying something and doing something else have been forbidden, which shows how practical the teachings of the Quran are, because it is mostly the smaller mistakes that create huge problems among people.

ETTIQUETTE There are some quotations about good and decent behaviour which hold good even today. They are given below:

> Surah 24 verses 27 – 29 "Believers, do not enter the dwellings of other men until you have asked their owners' permission and wished them peace. That will be best for you. Perchance you will take heed. If you find no one in them do not go in till you are given leave. If you are refused admission, it is but right that you should go away. Allah has knowledge of all your actions. It shall be no offence for you to seek shelter in empty dwellings, where you have some of your belongings. Allah knows what you hide and what you reveal."

Surah 24 verse 58 "Believers, let your slaves and children ask your leave when they come in to see you before the morning prayer, when you have put off your garments in the heat of noon and after the evening prayer. These are the three occasions when none may intrude upon you."

Surah 24 verse 60 When you enter a house, salute one another in the name of Allah, and let your greeting be devout and kindly."

Surah 33 verses 53 –54 "Believers do not enter the houses of the Prophet for a meal without waiting for the proper time, unless you are given leave. But if you are invited, enter; and when you have eaten, disperse. Do not engage in familiar talk, for this would annoy the Prophet and he would be ashamed to bid you go; but of the truth Allah is not ashamed."

Surah 49 verse 4 "Those who call out to you [Mohammad] whilst you are in your chambers are for the most part foolish men. If they waited until you went out to them it would be better for them. But Allah is forgiving and merciful." These instructions were mainly for the uneducated Arabs of the Prophet's time but if we ponder on them in detail, they are useful for everyone and help to maintain good relations and avoid misunderstandings.

BUSINESS TRANSACTIONS Quotations regarding trade and spending of money and giving alms are also many. Some are given below.

Surah 2 verse 282 Believers when you contract a debt for a fixed period, put it in writing."

Surah 2 verse 280 If your debtor be in straits, grant him a delay until he can discharge his debt; but if you waive the sum as alms it will be better for you, if you but knew it.

Surah 7 verse 85 "Give just weight and measure and do not defraud others of their possessions."

Surah 11 verse 85 '[Prophet Shoaib said] My people give just weight and measure and do not defraud others of their possessions and do not corrupt the land with evil.'

Surah 17 verse 35 "Give full measure when you measure, and weigh with even scales. That is fair and better in the end."

EXPENDITURE AND ALMS GIVING The Quran gives many instructions about spending money properly and in a balanced way. People are enjoined to give as much alms as possible, without hardship to self. Following quotations are the important ones about expenditure of money properly.

Surah 17 verse 26 –29 "Give to the near of kin their due, and also to the destitute and to the wayfarers. Do not squander your substance wastefully for the wasteful are

Satan's brother and Satan is ever ungrateful to his Lord. But if while waiting for your Lord's bounty, you lack the means to assist them, then atleast speak to them kindly. Be neither miserly nor prodigal, for then you should either be reproached or be reduced to penury."

Surah 104 veres 1 –4 Woe to all back biting slanderers who amass riches and sedulously hoard them, thinking their treasures will render them immortal! By no means! They shall be flung to the Destroying Flame."

Surah 3 verse 92 You shall never be truly righteous until you give in alms what you dearly cherish. The alms you give are known to Allah."

Surah 2 verse 263 –265 "A kind word with forgiveness is better than charity followed by insult. Allah is self sufficient and indulgent. Believers do not mar your almsgiving with taunts and mischief making, like those who spend their wealth for the sake of ostentation and believe neither in Allah nor in the Last Day. Such men are like a rock covered with earth : a shower falls upon it and leaves it hard and bare. They shall gain nothing from their works. Allah does not guide the unbelievers. But those that give away their wealth from a desire to please Allah and to reassure their own souls are like a garden on a hill side : if a shower falls upon it, it yields up twice its normal crop, and if no rain falls upon it, it is watered by the dew [which is sufficient for it]. Allah takes cognizance of all your actions."

Surah 2 verse 267 "Believer give in alms of the wealth you have lawfully earned and of that which We have brought out of the earth for you; not worthless things which you yourselves would only reluctantly accept. Know that Allah is self sufficient and glorious."

Surah 2 verse 271 "To be charitable in public is good, but to give alms to the poor in private is better and will atone for some of your sin. Allah has knowledge of all your actions."

Surah 24 verse 22 "Let the rich and honourable among you not swear to withhold their gifts from their kindred, the poor and those who have fled their homes for the cause of Allah. Rather let them pardon and forgive. Do you not wish Allah to forgive you? He is forgiving and merciful" This verse has a specific backgroud which should be mentioned here. Some Muslims had spread wrong rumours about the Prophet's wife Bibi Ayesha and so her father Hazrat Abu Baker swore to withhold his monetary help to them. Allah tells him to forgive and forget.

Surah 30 verse 38 –39 "Give their due to the near of kin, to the needy, and to the wayfarers. That is best for those that strive to please Allah; such men will surely prosper. That which you seek to increase by usury will not be blessed by Allah; but the alms you give for His sake shall be repaid to you many times over." In this quotation Allah says that you actually owe money to the needy from your wealth, because Allah has blessed you with riches, its your duty to help the unfortunate. In another place Allah says that He tests people by giving them riches: to see whether they give alms or not. Secondly Allah says do not be afraid that by distributing your riches among the poor and needy you will become poor. No. If you spend to please Allah, He will give you many times over. On the other hand if you are miserly and horde your wealth or seek to double it through usury [which Allah has forbidden] you will not prosper because Allah will not bless your wealth. It is said in the Quran that Satan frightens you with the possibility of destitution and Allah encourages you with promise of prosperity; so don't hesitate in spending for the needy. The main idea in encouraging alms giving is to reduce the gap between the rich and the poor and prevent accumulation of wealth among a few. This is the principle which is being adopted through different means by many countries in their national planning in modern times; India being one of them.

There are many more quotations about conducting business and trade by fair means and being honest and just in all transactions and being generous. In all the above quotations where the word 'believers' is used it need not mean only Muslims but all those who believe in a Supreme Being and His judgement of mankind. Giving alms only for show without a will to please God or to taunt the receiver is condemned, which appeals to reason. All these injunctions hold good in the present times.

SOCIAL EVILS AND FORBIDDEN BEHAVIOUR

The Quran comments on the various social evils that plague the society even today, like drunkenness, gambling, prostitution, infanticide, specially female infanticide, stealing, cheating and murder. Rules are laid down for punishment of various crimes in this world, while all wrong doers are warned again and again of eternal punishment in the Hereafter, if they do not repent and give up wrong doing. Certain acts, besides the obvious crimes are also forbidden in the Quran. Some of them appear very insignificant, may be because people indulge in them most of the time, but if we ponder on them, even those small bad acts can cause a lot of trouble, hence they are forbidden. Some important quotations regarding the social evils are given below. The worst and unforgivable sin according to the Quran is to equate some other being with the Supreme Being. Allah says He will not forgive this sin, unless the sinner truly repents. This applies to all humanity because the real model of Hanif [believer in One God] as mentioned in the Quran is the Patriarch Abraham. There are two important quotations in this regard. Surah 4 verse 48 "Allah will not forgive those who serve other gods beside Him; but He will forgive whom He will for other sins. He that serves other gods besides Him is guilty of a heinous sin." Surah 4 verse 116 "Allah will not forgive idolatory. He will forgive whom He will all other sins. He that serves other gods besides Allah has strayed far from the truth." Recent research has shown that people who believe in One God and trust Him are more satisfied and stress free than people who believe in gods other than the One Supreme Being who is worshipped in all religions. [Times of India, May 2008]

Surah 2 verse 219 "They ask you about drinking and gambling. Say 'There is great harm in both, although they have some benefit for men; but their harm is far greater than their benefit." [Both acts have been forbidden by Allah as the following quotation shows.]

Surah 5 verse 90 : "Believers wine and games of chance [gambling] idols and divining arrows, are abominations devised by Satan. Avoid them, so that you may prosper."

Surah 2 verse 275 "Those that live on usury shall rise up before Allah like men whom Satan has demented by his touch; for they claim that usury is like trading. But Allah has permitted trading and forbidden usury."

Surah 5 verse 38 "As for the man or woman who is guilty of theft, cut off their hands to punish them for their crimes. That is the punishment enjoined by Allah. He is mighty and Wise."

Surah 24 verse 2 "The adulterer and the adulteress shall each be given a hundred lashes." Surah 24 verse 4 "Those that defame honourable women and cannot produce four witnesses shall be given eighty lashes."

Surah 24 verse 33 "You shall not force your slave girls into prostitution in order that you may make money, if they wish to preserve their chastity. If any one compels them, Allah will be forgiving and merciful to them [slave girls]." This shows the humane aspect of Quranic law, that although prostitution is strictly prohibited, a slave girl who is forced to it, will be forgiven by Allah.

INFANTICIDE AND MURDER

Since this is a crime deserving capital punishment and

unfortunately has become quite common in modern times, quotations regarding it are being given separately.

Surah 17 veres 31 – 33 "You shall not kill your children for fear of want. We will provide for them and for you. To kill them is a great sin. You shall not commit adulery, for it is foul and indecent. You shall not kill any man whom Allah has forbidden you to kill, except for a just cause. If a man is slain unjustly his heir is entitled to satisfaction. But let him not carry his vengeance too far, for his victim will in turn be assisted and avenged." There are many more verses forbidding murder and Quran repeats the teaching of the Bible that he who saves a life saves all humanity and he who kills a life wantonly kills the entire humanity. Even in war, killing of innocents, women and children is forbidden.. [details of this will be covered in a later chapter on Jehad] Killing of children, mainly girls is an evil practice which was followed in many societies due to various reasons and unfortunately it is being practised in our country even today. In this regard the following quotations are relevent.

Surah 6 verse 140 "Lost are those that in their ignorance have wantonly slain their own children and made unlawful what Allah has given them, inventing falsehoods about Allah."

There are a couple of verses forbidding female infanticide specially, and we are aware how relevant it is in the present day!

Surah 16 verses 58- 59 "When the birth of a girl is announced to one of them, his face grows dark and he is filled with inward gloom. Because of the bad news he hides himself from men : should he keep her with disgrace or bury her under the dust [earth]? How ill they judge'.

Surah 81 verses 8 –9 "When [on the day of Judgement] the infant girl buried alive, is asked for what crime she was slain?

EVIL PRACTICES

Some common practices which cause a lot of trouble are also forbidden, like rumour mongering, slandering, back biting spying on private affairs of others, doubting the word of others unnecessarily and so on. The following quotations are given to explain better.

Surah 4 verse 83 "When they hear any news, good or bad, they at once make it known to all and sundry; whereas if they reported it to the apostle and to their own leaders[it would have been better], those who sought news could learn it from them."

Surah 17 verses 36 – 38 Do not follow what you do not know. Men's eyes ears and heart – each of his senses shall be closely questioned. Do not walk proudly on earth. You cannot cleave the earth, nor can you rival the mountain in stature. All this is evil; odious in the sight of your Lord."

Surah 49 verse 6 "Believers, if an evil doer brings you a piece of news inquire first into its truth, lest you should wrong others unwittingly and then repent of what you have done."

Surah 49 verse 12 "Believers, avoid immoderate suspicion, for in some cases suspicion is a crime. Do not spy on one another, nor back bite one another. Would any of you like to eat the flesh of his dead brother? Surely you would loath it. Have fear of Allah. He is forgiving and merciful."

Surah 57 verse 24 "Allah does not love the haughty, the vainglorious; nor those who being niggardly themselves, enjoin others to be niggardly also." These quotations show how distasteful to Allah are the common evil practices in which we indulge quite often without thinking. If we avoid them life would become much easier for all.

The Quran gives detailed instructions and rules about marriage, divorce, inheritance, conditions of war, treaties and establishment of peace and so on. These are all related to daily life and are relevant for all times but since these are a part of Islamic Shariat [code of conduct] they are followed by Muslims alone hence they are not being discussed here. They will be discussed in later chapters.

SOLACE AND PEACE OF MIND Today life has become so stressful that everyone seeks peace of mind and solace. People resort to Yoga and meditation to find peace. The Quran also offers solace and peace of mind through its teachings. Many of its verses explain how life is temporary and profit and loss or ups and downs are natural. They are all controlled by the Supreme Being and man has no control over it so there is no use lamenting over misfortunes. Similarly Quran explains that those who seek God's help and guidance will learn to bear their losses and misfortunes with fortitude. Some relevent quotations are being given below.

Surah 2 verse 45 –46 "Fortify yourself with patience and prayer. This may indeed be an exacting discipline, but not to the devout, who know that they will meet their Lord and that to Him they will return."

Surah 3 verses 139 – 140 "Take heart and do not despair. Have faith and you shall triumph. If you have suffered a defeat so did the enemy We alternate these viccisitudes among mankind so that Allah may know the true believers."

Surah 3 verse 160 "If Allah helps you none can overcome you. If He abandons you, who then can help you?"

Surah 7 verse 196 "He is the guardian of the righteous."

Surah 9 verse 40 "If you do not help him [Mohammad], Allah will help him as He helped him when he was driven out by the unbelievers with one other. In the cave he said to his companion : Do not despair Allah is with us. Allah caused His tranquility to descend upon him and sent to his aid invisible warriors, so that the [word of] unbelievers was routed and the Word of Allah was exalted" Although this verse is about a specific occasion in the life of the prophet

Mohammad, it provides strength to believers, in their time of need that God will help them as long as they are on the right path.

Surah 9 verse 51 "Say : Nothing will befall us except what Allah has ordained. He is our Guardian In Allah let the faithful put their trust."

Surah 10 verse 107 "If Allah afflicts you with a misfortune none can remove it but He; and if He bestows on you a favour, none can withhold His bounty. He is bountiful to whom He will."

Surah 13 verse 28 'Those who believe, and whose hearts find satisfaction in the remembrance of Allah: for without doubt in the remembrance of Allah do hearts find satisfaction.'

Surah 22 verse 60" He that repays an injury in kind and then is wronged again shall be helped by Allah. Allah is merciful and forgiving."

Surah 27 verse 62 "Surely worthier is He who answers the oppressed when they cry out to Him and relieves their affliction."

Surah 39 verse 36 'Is not Allah enough for His servant? But they try to frighten thee with other [gods] beside Him! For such as Allah leaves to stray, there can be no guide.'

Surah 39 verse 52 "Do they not know that Allah gives abundantly to whom He will, and paringly to whom He pleases? Surely there are signs in this for true believers."

Surah 57 verses 22 – 23 "Every misfortune that befalleth the earth, or your own persons, is ordained before We bring it into being. That is easy for Allah: so that you may not grieve for the good things you miss or be overjoyed at what you gain."

Surah 64 verse 11 "No misfortune befalls except by Allah'

will. He guides the hearts of those who believe in Him. Allah has knowledge of all things."

Surah 65 verse 2 "He that fears Allah, Allah will give him a means of salvation and provide for him whence he does not reckon: Allah is all sufficient for the man who puts his trust in Allah. He will surely bring about what He decrees. He has set a measure for all things." This verse is a great solace for the believers in divine mercy, what ever faith they follow. The Almighty reassures the person who puts his faith and trust in Him and promises him salvation and deliverance from all difficulties.

Surah 70 verses 19–21 "Indeed man was created impatient. When evil befalls him he is despondent; but blessed with good fortune he grows niggardly." This verse teaches us about human nature, and also teaches us to try and overcome it. When we are in trouble we should not give up hope but be positive and constructive and ask for divine help and guidance, similarly when we are blessed by the Lord we should praise Him, be thankful to Him and share our good fortune with others.

Surah 94 veres 1–8 "Have We not lifted up your [Mohammad's] heart and relieved you of the burden which weighed down your back? Have We not given you high renown ? Every hardship is followed by ease. Every hardship is followed by ease. When your task is ended resume your toil, and seek your Lord with all fervour." Once again this entire Surah is addressed to the prophet but has a message and lesson for any one who pays heed to it. There are many more verses in the Quran which provide solace and reasurance to people, specially when they are disheartened or frustrated.

We have tried to show with the help of Quranic quotations, how relevant the teachings and injunctions of the Quran are in modern times. In fact the teachings of all

Holy Scriptures are basically the same and hence are relevant for all times and people who follow them in principle and in the true spirit always benefit through them, be they followers of any religious tradition.

References

1. N J Dawood The Koran A Translation Allen Lane London.
2. Mohd. M Pickthall Holy Quran English Translation.

4

Characteristics of a Good Believer

A good believer need not be only a Muslim but he may be professor of any faith because the Quran says, "Believers, Jews, Christians and Sabaean-whoever believes in Allah [Supreme Being] and in the Last Day [Day of Judgement] and does what is right-shall be rewarded by their Lord – they have nothing to fear or regret. [Surah 2 verse 62] The Quran further explains the traits of a good believer and also enjoins all believers to become true servants of their Lord and surrender their will to Him. Other Holy scriptures also explain the traits of good believers and they are similar because the Truth is universal and the message of the Supreme Being has always been the same. Good deeds have been enumerated in detail in the Bible in the Gospel in the Bhagvad Gita and in other Holy Books. The sign of believers are also mentioned in similar words in all the above scriptures and some examples were quoted in an earlier chapter. Quran is a reminder for all mankind and the last message from the Supreme Being. In this Chapter we will concentrate on Quranic quotations about good believers and their qualities.

The Quran mentions again and again that all those who do good will be rewarded by Allah, both in this world and the next. Not only this, the Quran also says that if you do good and avoid doing bigger sins, Allah will forgive your lesser sins and be merciful to you. The Quran explains very clearly what are the good acts which should be performed by the believers.

Allah does not ask people to become ascetics and give up worldly pleasures but enjoins them to do every thing in a proper way as taught by their scriptures and always to maintain a balance in what ever they do. Thus the Quran gives details about social relations and behaviour, economic activities, rules of marriage, divorce and inheritance and so on as mentioned in the previous chapter. In this chapter we will concentrate on the specific instructions given to believers in Allah and the Day of Judgement, in order that they become true servants of their Lord. Now we will study about some Quranic quotations which mention the characteristics of true believers and for which all right thinking men and women should strive.

Surah 2 verse 277 'Those that have faith and do good works, attend to their prayers and pay the alms tax, will be rewarded by their Lord and will have nothing to fear or regret.'

Surah 3 verses 130 –136 "Believers do not live on usury, doubling your wealth many times over. Have fear of Allah, and you shall prosper. Guard yourself against the fire of Hell, prepared for unbelievers. Obey Allah and the Apostle that you may find mercy. Vie with each other to earn the forgiveness of your Lord and a Paradise as vast as heaven and earth, prepared for the righteous : those who give alms alike in prosperity and in adversity; who curb their anger and forgive their fellow men [Allah loves the charitable]; who, if they commit evil or wrong their souls, remember Allah and seek forgiveness of Him. [for who but Allah can forgive sin?] and do not knowingly persist in their misdeeds. These shall be regarded with forgiveness from their Lord and gardens watered by running streams, where they shall dwell for ever. Blessed is the reward of those who do good works."

Surah 4 verse 59 'Believers obey Allah and the Apostle and those in authority among you. Should you disagree about anything refer it to Allah and the Apostle, if you truly believe in Allah and the Last Day. This will in the end be better and more just.'

Surah 8 verses 3 –5 'Obey Allah and His apostle, if you are true believers. The true believers are those whose hearts are filled with awe at the mention of Allah, and whose faith grows stronger as they lissten to His revelations. They are those who put their trust in in their Lord, pray steadfastly, and bestow in alms of that which We have given them. Such are the true believers. They shall be exalted and forgiven by their Lord, and a generous provision shall be made for them.'

Surah 9 verse 71 "The true believers, both men and women, are friends to each other. They enjoin what is just[right] and forbid what is evil; they attend to their prayers and pay the alms tax and obey Allah and His apostle. On these Allah will have mercy. He is mighty and wise."

Surah 9 verses 111 - 112 'Allah has purchased of the faithful their lives and worldly goods and in return has promised them the Garden. They will fight for His cause, slay and be slain. Such is the true pledge which He has made them in the Torah, the Gospel and the Quran. And who is more true to his promise than Allah? Rejoice then in the bargain you have made. That is the supreme triumph. Those that repent and those that serve Allah and praise Him; those that fast and those that kneel and prostrate themselves before Him; those that enjoin justice, forbid evil and observe the commandments of Allah shall bc. richly rewarded.'

Surah 17 verse 20 "As for him that desires the life to come [eternal life] and strives for it with all his soul, being a true believer, his endeavours shall be rewarded by Allah."

Surah 22 verse 77 "You, that are true believers, kneel and prostrate yourselves. Worship your Lord and do good works, so that you may triumph."

Surah 23 verses 1–8 "Blessed are the believers, who are humble in their prayers, who avoid profane talk, and give alms to the destitute; who restrain their carnal desires [except with their wives and slave girls, for these are lawful to them] and do not transgress through lusting after other women; who are true to their trusts and promises and never neglect their prayers. These are the heirs of Paradise; they shall abide in it for ever." Very similar meaning is conveyed in Surah 70 verses 22 – 35. "Not so the worshippers who are steadfast in prayer; who set aside a due portion of their goods for the needy and the dispossesed; who truly believe in the Day of Reckoning and dread the punishment of their Lord [for none is secure from the punishment of their Lord]; who restrain their carnal desire [save with their wives and slave girls, for these are lawful to them: he that lusts after other than these is a transgressor]; who keep their trusts and promises and bear true witness; and who attend to their prayers with promptitude. These shall be laden with honours and shall dwell in fair gardens." These two quotations enumerate most of the traits of righteous men who believe in the Almighty. In other verses women are also included with men while describing the traits of believers. These verses are quoted in the Chapter on women. [Surah 33 verse 35]

Surah 30 veres 30 –32 "Therefore stand firm in your devotion to the true faith, which Allah Himself has made, and for which He has made man. Allah's creation cannot be changed. This is surely the true religion, although most men do not know it. Turn to Allah and fear Him. Be steadfast in prayer and serve no other god besides Him. Do not split up your religion into sects, each exulting in its own beliefs."

Surah 42 verse 35 "That which you have been given is but the fleeting comfort of this life. Better and more enduring is Allah's reward to to those who believe and put their trust in Him; who avoid gross sins and indecencies and, when angered, are willing to forgive; who obey their Lord, attend to their prayers, and conduct their affairs by mutual consent; who bestow in alms a part of that which We have given them and, when oppressed, seek to redress their wrongs." This quotation shows many characteristics of good believers and these have not only religious but also worldly significance. For instance it is said that the righteous control their anger and forgive; this is a very difficult practice although we all know that it is advisable. It is also said that when oppressed the righteous take revenge. This is a natural tendency and Allah allows it although forgiving is considered better, but in cases of injustice and oppression it is cowardly to keep quiet. One should raise one's voice against injustice and oppression.

Surah 47 verse 19 "Know that there is no god but Allah, Implore Him to forgive your sins and to forgive the true believers, men and women."

Surah 47 verse 33 "Believers, obey Allah and His apostle and never let your labour go in vain."

Surah 47 verse 36 "The life of this world is but a sport and a pastime. Allah will reward you if you believe in Him and guard yourselves against evil."

The believers have not only been asked to keep themselves on the right path but also enjoined to guide their families to be righteous. The Prophet has also been asked in some verses to be kind to those close to him and also to guide them. The following quote admonishes the believers to protect themselves and their kin from Allah' wrath [by avoiding evil and being righteous].

Surah 66 verse 6 "Believers guard yourselves and guard your kindred against the Fire which has fuel of men and stones, whose keepers are fierce and mighty angels who never disobey Allah's command and promptly do His bidding." This verse shows that it is the duty of the head of the family to teach the right behaviour and faith to his family. Ofcourse he can do this only if he himself is following the right path. He can best teach by precept rather than by preaching; but there is need to read the Quran and also encourage family members to read and understand the teaching of the Quran and then put them into practice. If we think deeply this is a very big and important responsibility of all believers and if everyone were to shoulder it seriously, most of the problems and difficulties in life would disappear of their own accord.

There are many verses in the Quran which are prayers meant for the God fearing. One of these, which is a comprehensive prayer, and also specifies the characteristics of the true believers, is being quoted here. It is specially meant for believers and includes the Prophet as their leader.

Surah 2 verses 285 –286 "The Apostle believes in what has been revealed to him by his Lord., and so do the faithful. They all believe in Allah and His angels, His scriptures, and His apostles: We discriminate against none of His apostles. They say:" We hear and obey. Grant us your forgivenesss, Lord; to You we shall all return. Allah does not charge a soul with more than it can bear. It shall be requited for whatever good and what ever evil it has done. Lord, do not be angry with us if we forget or lapse into error. Lord, do not lay on us the burden You laid on those before us. Lord, do not charge us with more than we can bear. Pardon us, forgive us our sins, and have mercy upon us. You alone are our Protector. Give us victory over the unbelievers." This is a very comprehensive prayer and represents the general pattern of prayers in the Quran. Man is expected to first praise the Lord, express his obedience and his allegience to Him and then ask for His mercy and special favours. In this prayer the believers also express their belief in all prophets without any distinction among them, as does the last Apostle of God. They also express their belief in all the basic tenets of the true faith, namely ISLAM in Arabic language.

There are many verses in the Quran which describe the rewards that would be bestowed upon the believers who are also righteous. Mainly, their reward is Heaven which has been described in countless verses; while the entire Surah Rahman is focused on the description of the Gardens of Heaven it also repeatedly admonishes the reader not to refute the bounties of Allah. Even in this world the believers have been assured of Allah's blessings and guidance. Due to their faith, they are content with what Allah has given them and do not covet others' riches. Satisfaction with one's status, contentment and submission to Allah's will are qualities which bring mental peace and keep men free of tension and dissatisfaction. This itself is a big reward in the modern world. The Quran says that whoever has been delivered from the evil promptings of one's Nafs [self], is really successful. Now we shall present some quotations about the rewards of the good believers.

Surah 47 verse 7 "As for those who are slain in the cause of Allah, He will not allow their works to perish. He will vouchafe them guidance and ennoble their state; He will admit them to the Paradise He has made known to them."

Surah 47 verse 12 "Allah will admit those who embrace the true faith and do good works to garden watered by running streams.

Surah 47 verse 15 "This is the Paradise which the righteous have been promised. There shall flow in it rivers of unpolluted water and rivers of milk forever fresh; rivers of delectable wine and rivers of clearest honey. They shall eat therein of every fruit and receive forgiveness from their Lord." Paradise has been described countless times and is said to contain all types of luxuries and comforts, but the main achievement for the righteous will be that in the Paradise they will be blessed by the Lord, their sins will be forgiven and Allah will be pleased with them and they will be pleased with Allah. This is the highest bliss for a human being and such a person is said to be Nafs e Mutmainna. [satisfied self]

In the Quran it has been proclaimed again and again that if people believe in Allah and repent of their misdeeds, Allah will definitely forgive them. He is the Most Merciful. There is hope for even the worst sinner, except that he has to repent sincerely and ask for Allah's forgiveness and then do good deeds. He will not be forgiven if all his life he remained an unbeliever and only at the time of death says that he repents. This is what Pharoah had done and was punished. The following quotations show that Allah does not punish people unless they commit really dreadful sins.

Surah 4 verse 147 "And why should Allah punish you if you render thanks to Him and truly believe in Him, Allah will reward your labours for He knows them all."

Surah 8 verse 53 'Allah does not withhold His favours from men until they change what is in their hearts. Allah hears all and knows all.'

Surah 11 verse 117 'Your Lord would not have ruined those cities, with out just cause, had their inhabitants been righteous men.' These verses show that Allah is Most Merciful and at the same time Most Just. He would not punish people without cause. If men and women believe in Him and surrender to His Will, they have nothing to fear, either in this world or the next. There is always scope for repenting and asking for God's forgiveness and starting afresh, because God is also Most Forgiving and Kind.

The Quran is very practical in its approach and in the case of punishment, specially in this world, it is said that fear the punishment which will not be confined only to the wrong doers but will affect all people residing in that area. Therefore the precaution that can be taken is that everyone should try to be righteous and also try to prevent others from doing wrong and encourage them to do good by explaining to them in a friendly manner and also by setting a good example. Its also said in the Quran that generally it is the rich and mighty in a country who start disobeying the Lord and then everyone in that area has to face the consequences, so such leaders should also be warned by the righteous. The biggest problem today is who can be defined as the righteous to shoulder this great responsibility? Many people preach but do not set a precept, or those who are good examples have no public authority to influence people and most of all no one is bothered about the moral welfare of the society. Of course this is quite disappointing but if everyone tries to be good on his own and try to keep his family on the right path a lot of moral progress would definitely result.

TRANSLATIONS

1. Mohd. M Pickthall Holy Quran English Translation.
2. N.J. Dawood 1978, The Koran A Translation Allen Lane London.
3. Abdullah Yusuf Ali The Holy Quran English Translation Adam Publishers 2007.

5

Women in Islam

The status of women in Islam is a hotly debated topic for the intelligentsia all over the world and generally it is felt that women have a lower status in Islam and are controlled by their men folk. What I would like to ask is in which religion or society is the case different? All religious books and scriptures give men a higher position than women and also give reasons for it. Considering this book aims to view Islam as the universal religion, it is only logical to agree that since men and women are differently made the Supreme Being has allotted different roles and statuses for both of them and proclaimed this in all divine messages to humanity, since earliest times, as it has been finally proclaimed in the Quran, too. Let us also remember that in every society women are given a lower position than men and are controlled by them, even today, although legally and theoretically they have been granted equal rights by many nation. As Indu Menon writes,.Human history reveals that woman was granted a low status in most civilizations since ancient times. In the Puranic Hindu period women were treated as quite inferior beings. In Christianity and Judaism woman was considered a source of temptation and evil. In Buddhism salvation was denied to those who consorted with women. In Greece, Rome, Egypt and China woman was generally considered just a domestic drudge; to stay at home and mind the house was her only recognized role.[1] True, in modern times women are becoming more independent and protesting against male control but gender equality is yet a dream and women are facing new problems and discriminations. I am a strong believer in women's rights and their empowerment but I also believe that men and women complement each other and need to play their respective roles in society to maintain social order. Gender equality is an ideal which probably will remain so because literal equality is neither practical nor advisable. Instead we should talk of gender sensitivity and gender justice, so that women are not exploited or treated like commodity. When we adopt this view we see that Islam offers a satisfactory and realistic position to women. Of course some injunctions might seem unfavourable to women from a feminist point of view, but they carry a lot of common sense and are akin to reality. Here it is relevant to quote a famous saying of the great thinker, Aristotle who said, 'the worst form of inequality is to try and make equal, two things which are unequal.' Many authors have written in different contexts that men and women are complementary and not literally equal, so they should be treated as such and not treated as exactly similar. Margaret Mead has written in Male and Female, "Every adjustment that minimizes a difference, a vulnerability, in one sex, a differential strength in the other, diminishes their possibility of complementing each other and corresponds symbolically to sealing off the constructive receptivity of the female and the vigorous outgoing constructive activity of the male, muting them both in the end to duller versions of human life in which each is denied the fullness of humanity that each might have had. Guard each sex in its vulnerable moments, but as we guard we must also keep the differences. Simply compensating for differences is in the end a form of denial."[2] In this regard the Quranic quotation that appears relevant is as follows:

Surah 4 verse 34 'Men have authority over women because Allah has made the one superior to the others, and because they spend their wealth to maintain them.' Another quotation from the Quran enjoins women not to hanker after the position and power given to men but be satisfied with the position and power given to them as women, because both sexes have their own importance.

Surah 4 verse 32 'Do not covet the favours by which Allah has exalted some of you above others. Men as well as women shall be rewarded for their labours. Rather implore Allah to bestow on you His gifts. Allah has knowledge of all things.' Islam grants an honourable position to women in society, as will be shown by Quranic quotations later, keeping the basic realities and potentialities of males and females in view.

In fact, Islam has given many rights to women, that were not given to them by earlier religions, because as Allah says the Quran has been sent to remove various burdens from mankind which had oppressed them earlier, but at the same time Islam gives women a lower position than men. Nevertheless it treats women as equal to men when it comes to matters of faith, religious obligations and reward for good deeds and punishment for bad deeds. Islam gives property rights to women just as it gives to men, although women get lesser share than men. It enjoins both men and women to acquire education, both religious and secular. It gives women right to do business independently. Before the advent of Islam the status of women in Arabia was very low as it was elsewhere in those times. A woman had no recognised place as an individual in pre- Islamic Arab society. She belonged to her menfolk. The birth of a daughter was looked upon as a disgrace and female infanticide was a common practice. If a girl was allowed to live she was married off at an early age. A man could marry any number of wives and divorce them at will any number of times without letting them free. Islam improved the position of women in many ways by making new provisions for women's rights and welfare in the Quran.

The following Ayats from the Quran reveal the injunctions and orders about status and treatment of women in Islam.

Surah 4 verse 7 Unto the men [of a family] belongeth a share of that which parents and near kindred leave, and unto the women a share of that which parents and near kindred leave, whether it be little or much - a legal share.

Surah 4 verse 34 "Men have authority over women because Allah has made the one superior to the others, and because they spend their wealth to maintain them. Good women are obedient. They guard their unseen parts because Allah has guarded them [in the absence of their husbands] As for those from whom you fear disobedience, admonish them and send them to beds apart and beat them. Then if they obey you, take no action against them. Allah is high, supreme."

Surah 2 verse 223 "Women are your fields: go, then, into your fields as you please. Do good works and fear Allah."

Surah 2 verse 187 'They [women] are raiment for you and you [men] are raiment for them

Surah 2 verse 228 And they [women] have rights similar to those [of men] over them [men] in kindness.'

Surah 4 verse 124 'And whoso doeth good works, whether of male or female, and he or she is a believer, such will enter Paradise and they will not be wronged the dint in a date stone.'

Sura 4 verse 19 'Consort with them [wives] in kindness, for if you dislike a thing in them it may happen that you dislike a thing wherein Allah has placed much good.'

All these quotations show that in Islam both male and female are equally answerable to Allah for their actions and will be rewarded equally. Both have legal and conjugal rights, although these rights are not equal as husbands, being protectors and providers, are granted a higher position. But women are said to excel in their own field over men. Women have been mentioned as good partners for men and good mothers who make many sacrifices and bear hardships for their children. These verses have a two fold purpose; they encourage women to be good wives and mothers and encourage men and children to realize the importance of women and treat them kindly and with respect. The quotations are being given below:

Surah 30 verse 21 'By another sign He gave you wives from among yourselves, that you may live in joy with them, and planted love and kindness in your hearts. Surely in this there are signs for thinking men.'

Surah 46 verse 15 'We have enjoined man to show kindness to his parents. With much pain his mother bears him, and with much pain she brings him into the world. He is born and weaned in thirty months. When he grows to manhood and attains his fortieth year, let him say: 'Inspire me Lord to give thanks for the favours You have bestowed on me and on my parents, and to do good works that will please you. Grant me good descendants. To You I turn and to You I surrender myself.'

The teachings of the Quran are reinforced by the Sayings of Prophet Mohammad, with regard to women. Some of his famous sayings in favour of women are as follows.

'Paradise is at the feet of the mother.'

'It is the generous [in character] who are good to women and it is the wicked who insult them.'

'Whosoever has a daughter and he has not buried her alive, does not insult her, and does not prefer his son to her, God will enter him into Paradise.'

It is true that the Quran does not regard women as equal to men in some ways. For instance in case of bearing witness it has been said, in one Quranic verse that if two men are not available then one man and two women may be regarded as witnesses for money transactions, i.e. two women in place of another man. [Surah 2 verse 282] but in other places where witnesses are mentioned, there is no specification about male or female, specially in Surah 24 verse 6 it is said that each spouse can be a witness in case of adultery by the other, so some commentators say that women are not considered inferior to men always, only in the case of money transaction it has been said so. Secondly women are given half the share of men in parental property. Here also commentators write that in Islam men have many monetary responsibilities while women have none so men are given double the share generally, while some times women get more than half the share. In marriage also men have the permission to marry up to four women at a time if they so desire but a woman can only marry one man. This again is a universally prevalent practice, with some exceptions among primitive tribes. Most modern women may not like polygamy but many are forced to tolerate it because even today. although monogamy is the norm in all societies, men continue to have extra marital affairs and marry more than one woman, quite often. Islam considers adultery a major crime therefore it allowed men to marry more than one woman if they are not satisfied with one wife, but the Quran too, favours monogamy. Besides these inequalities, in one place in the Quran, two weaknesses of women are pointed out as follows:

> Surah 43 verses 16 –19 'Yet they assign to Him offspring from among His servants! Surely man is monstrously ungrateful. Would Allah choose daughters for Himself and sons for you? Yet when the birth of a daughter is announced to one of them his face darkens and he is filled with gloom. Would they ascribe to Allah females who adorn themselves with trinkets and are powerless in disputation.'

While the last part sounds discriminatory towards women and may not apply to all women, it is also true to quite some extent, in the case of most women, because women are in general more interested in frivolous things than intellectual pursuits. On the other hand the verse denounces the practice of lamenting a daughter's birth, a common practice in contemporary society. Even today, with all the education and women's emancipation, couples want to have sons rather than daughters the world over. The heinous practices of female infanticide and female foeticide [both prohibited in the Quran] are on the increase in the modern society. Various customs and traditions are responsible for keeping women ignorant and illiterate and considering them as a burden for their men folk, which make women diffident and unable to express and argue coherently. While it is wrong to exploit women in this way, it is also not possible to treat them as literally equal to men in every way. Even post feminist theories are now accepting to value the differences between men and women, realising it is the interpretation of gender roles that makes men and women unequal, not the roles themselves. This is very close to what Islam pronounces; i.e. both women and men have to play their own roles which are equally important

Many authors have commented on the fact that Islam has improved the status of women. Kapadia writes that Islam improved the status of women by restricting polygyny to four wives and by favouring monogamy, as mentioned in Quran 4:3, [because in pre Islamic Arabia men married countless women] by condemning female infanticide, by assigning share in inheritance, by declaring Mehr as a compulsory gift to the bride and by reorienting the Arab law of marriage and divorce in favour of women like providing maintenance [during iddat period] to divorced women and to the children. Paradise was promised to a believing woman as it was to a believing man. Woodsmall writes, 'there is little doubt that the Prophet was inspired by the ideal of elevating the position of women of his day - his teachings represent a social reform movement against existing practices, which was very significant for that day and included such measures as the abolition of infanticide, limitation of polygyny, protection of widows and orphans, marriage contract, the granting of marriage dowry [Mehr] and inheritance rights to women. Shushtery writes that Islam contributed to the status improvement of women in the following ways: [1] by stressing the need to respect and to give good treatment to a foster mother, [2] by making woman the mistress of her own property in which the husband had no right to interfere except with her permission., [3] by giving her the right of claiming divorce [khula], [4] by allowing her to hold any public office, [5] by giving her the freedom to remarry after divorce, and [6] by encouraging her to study and acquire knowledge.[3]

Muslim scholars like Ameer Ali, Mohammad Qutb, Sir Syed Ahmad Khan and Prof. Mujeeb have all written about the equal status offered to men and women in religion and law, although both Sir Syed and Prof. Mujeeb lament that in practice women are not given all the rights that should be given to them. This is because of the patriarchal social system prevalent in all societies. Mohammad Qutb writes, "Islam holds that woman is a human being and has a soul similar to that of man. Men and women are equal in their origin, their abode and their place of return, and are as such entitled to similar and equal rights. Islam gives her the right to life, to honour and to property like men.' Siddiqui explains the concept of equality of sexes in Islam in detail. He says there is a specific sex individuality in man and woman which each must preserve and cherish, because it gives them honour and dignity and enables them to fulfill in an effective manner their specific roles in society. Consistent with this specific individuality, both sexes have equal rights and are distinct legal personalities. According to Islamic law a wife is a separate legal person and can sue her husband if he denies her any legal rights. This position was not accorded to her in the teachings of earlier apostles and in the West women got such rights in the secular sphere only after a lot of struggle and that too, only in modern times. The legal position of a married woman was the merging of her individuality with that of her husband.[4]

The Quran also forbids men to use their female slaves for prostitution and also promises forgiveness to those female slaves who are forced into it against their will.

Surah 24 verse 33 'You shall not force your slave girls into prostitution in order that you may make money, if they wish to presérve their chastity. If any one compels them, Allah will be forgiving and merciful to them.' This shows the extent to which Allah is compassionate towards dependent women.

The concept of Hijab or Purdah if understood and practised properly, does not restrict a Muslim woman from doing anything that she has been allowed to do by religion, like acquiring education, doing business or working outside home. In fact it protects her from evil eyes and evil designs. In this regard Islam has laid down rules in the Quran for preserving modesty among women. Here again it has to be mentioned that there are rules for men also to preserve modesty in dress and department. Just as women are asked to lower their gaze when accosted by strangers, men also are asked not to stare at women but lower their gaze. Both men and women have been forbidden to indulge in promiscuous behaviour and. the punishment for adultery is the same for men and women. Two famous quotations about Hijab are given below:

> Surah 24 verse 31 'Enjoin believing women to turn their eyes away from temptation and to preserve their chastity; to cover their adornments [except such as are normally displayed]; to draw their veils over their bosoms and not to reveal their finery except to their husbands, their fathers, their husbands' fathers, their sons, their step-sons, their brothers, their brothers' sons, their sisters' sons, their women servants, and their slave girls; male attendants lacking in natural vigour, and children who have no carnal knowledge of women. And let them not stamp their feet in walking so as to reveal their hidden trinkets.'

Surah 33 verse 59 'Prophet! Enjoin your wives, your daughters and the wives of true believers to draw their covers close around them. That is more proper so that they may be recognised and not molested. Allah is forgiving and merciful.'

Some more injunctions about modesty and reserve in behaviour have been addressed to the wives of the Prophet but they apply to all believing women. These are quoted below.

Surah 33 verse 53 "If you ask his [prophet's] wives for anything, speak to them from behind a curtain. This is more chaste for your hearts and their hearts.'

Surah 33 verses 32- 33 Wives of the prophet! you are not like other women. If you fear Allah do not be too complaisant in your speech, lest the lecherous-hearted should lust for you Show discretion in what you say. Stay in your homes and do not display your finery as women used to do in the days of ignorance. Attend to your prayers, give alms to the poor, and obey Allah and His apostle.'

These quotations are also hotly debated and variously interpreted by different people. The basic injunction in these quotations is for women to dress modestly, cover their persons well when going out so as to look dignified and not become free with men. There is nothing wrong in following this because even in this modern time women are very vulnerable and have to be careful, specially in public to avoid harassment or molestation. Secondly, women have been asked not to go out unnecessarily in market places and other public places just to display their finery. This again is a very sensible injunction which is followed by decent women in all societies even today.

Some quotations which show that women are treated as equal to men in actions and rewards, are as follows:

> Surah 4 verse 124 'But the believers who do good works, whether men or women, shall enter the gardens of Paradise. They shall not suffer the least injustice.'

Surah 33 verse 35 'Those who surrender themselves to Allah and accept the true faith, who are devout, sincere, patient, humble, charitable and chaste; who fast and are ever mindful of Allah, on these, both men and women, Allah will bestow forgiveness and a rich reward.'

In many other places women's rights and status as independent individuals are clearly mentioned in the Quran. Women's rights with regard to property have been given in detail in Surah Nisa and their rights regarding marriage, family life and divorce are also explained and these will be discussed in detail in the next chapter. Here we need only comment that contrary to the general belief that Muslim women have no security in marriage as they may be divorced any time, Quran gives women the right to ask for a divorce, if they so desire and also does not permit men to divorce their wives off hand, instead it lays many rules and conditions for it. Anyway divorce is considered very undesirable and has been allowed only as a last resort. Secondly the Quran enjoins men to get those women married off who are single [lest they succumb to some temptation]. This applies to widows as well as divorced women. Thus the Quran gives women the right to remarry, in fact it encourages it. The relevant quotation is as follows:

> Surah 24 verse 32 'Marry those among you who are single, and the virtuous ones among your slaves, male or female.'

In conclusion we can say that while Quran does not subscribe to gender equality in toto, [which is not practical or viable] it treats women with honour and respect and gives them all those rights as human beings which are necessary for a person to operate as an independent individual.

TRANSLATIONS

N.J. Dawood 1978 The Koran A Translation Allen Lane London.
Abdullah Yusuf Ali The Holy Quran English Translation Adam Publishers.

References

1. Menon Indu 1981 Status of Muslim Women in India Uppal Publishing.
2. Rahman Zainab 2005, Women and Society, Kalpaz Publications.
3. Shushtery A M A 1938 Outlines of Islamic Culture.
4. Rahman Zainab 2000 'The Status of Women in Islam' in Muslim Women since Independence, Ed Hasina Hashia, Institute of Objective Studies New Delhi.

6

Marriage and Family in Islam

Marriage and family are two very important and primary institutions in any society. These are the institutions which regulate daily life and also propagate the human species. Sociologically too, they are of primary importance. Both these institutions have gone through different phases through human history as we learn in sociology and anthropology. While marriage is the accepted way of establishing sexual relations and setting up a home for a man and a woman, family is the accepted way of procreating and bringing up children, in a way that they become useful members of society. Every society has its own specific rules about these two institutions but basically their form and content are similar everywhere. In modern times, many changes have taken place in peoples' attitudes and ideas about these institutions and some revolutionary changes are noticed; for instance acceptance of same sex marriage and single parent family and so on. Still these are exceptions rather than the rule and are not accepted universally. All religious traditions have given great importance to marriage and family and provided rules and regulations for them. The main theme of this book being the universality of religion, we will point out that rules of marriage and functions of family are more or less similar in all religions and patriarchy is the accepted norm. Of course depending on the time and circumstances there are some variations in rules and regulations in different scriptures.

In the Quran too there are explicit injunctions and commandments about these two institutions. The Quran devotes many verses to explain the rules of marriage, the regulation of family life, the rights and obligations of different relatives towards each other, the conditions and rules of divorce, the rules of inheritance and so on. As seen in the previous chapter, the Quran also favours a patriarchal society and in marriage the man has a superior position than the wife although the wife has her own importance and rights in the family. The very fact that Allah created Eve for Adam, shows the importance of a mate for a human. This story has been repeated many times in the Quran, showing how Allah created Adam and Eve, who lived in Paradise at first and then were sent down to earth to live together and propogate their species. Thus marriage and setting up of family were the most important and basic aims of human existence.

First of all we will deal with the Quranic quotations about marriage, its importance, its rules and regulations and duties and rights of marriage partners.

Surah 4 verse 1 'O mankind ! Be dutiful to your Lord, who created you from a single person [Adam] and from him [Adam] He created his wife [Hawwa (Eve)], and from them both He created many men and women; and fear Allah through Whom you demand [your mutual rights] and [do not cut the relations of] wombs [kinship]. Surely Allah is Ever an All Watcher over you.'

Surah 16 verse 72 'And Allah has made for you wives of your own kind, and has made for you from your wives, sons and grand sons, and has bestowed on you good provision.'

Surah 25 verse 54 'And it is He, Who has created man from water, and has appointed for him kindred by blood and kindred by marriage.'

Surah 49 verse 13 'Men, We have created you from a male and a female and divided you into nations and tribes that you may get to know one another. The noblest of you in Allah's sight is he who fears Him most. Allah is Wise and all knowing.'

Surah 39 verse 6 'He created you from a single being, then from that being He created its mate He has given you four different pairs of cattle. He moulds you in your mothers' wombs by stages in three fold darkness.'

These quotations show how humanity was created by the union between a man and a woman, and then spread into families and tribes. The story of Adam and Eve, the first married couple in humanity, is repeated often in different Surahs of the Quran, as mentioned earlier, and stories of other married couples, showing instances from their life together, like those of Abraham and his wives, Moses and his wife, Lot and his wife, Job and his wife, Prophet Mohammad and his wives are also mentioned in the Quran. All these bring out the importance of leading a normal married life and rearing children as a duty towards humanity. In some older religious traditions celibacy had been glorified, hence the Quran explains that celibacy is not normal, instead it is normal to marry according to prescribed rules and set up families and nurture them. By giving examples of prophets, it is shown that all prophets were only human and lived normal lives. The following quotation makes it clearer: Surah 13 verse 38 'And indeed We sent messengers before you [O Mohammad] and made for them wives and offspring. And it was not for a messenger to bring a sign, except by Allah's Leave. [For] every matter there is a Decree [from Allah]

The rules of marriage are not given all together, at one place, in the Quran but at different places different rules and regulations are mentioned according to the relevant context. The important rules include the fixing of Mehr or Dower by the groom for the bride at the time of marriage, which he has to pay to his wife immediately or later; the presence of witnesses to the marriage contract being solemnised; the willingness of the bride and groom, or their guardians if they are underage, to contract the marriage and the formal proposal by the groom and the acceptance of the bride in front of the witnesses and the Vakil [person acting as trustee or guardian] of the bride. These rules have been elaborated upon by the Ahadith [sayings of the Prophet] The duties of husband and wife are also explained at different places in the Quran and are elaborated on by the Prophet PBUH, through his sayings. Now we will present some more quotations about marriage and accepted behaviour patterns for husbands and wives.

Surah 2 verse 223 'Women are your fields: go then into your fields as you please. Do good works for your own selves beforehand and fear Allah and know that you are to meet Him and give good tidings to believers [O Mohammad].'

Surah 2 verse 228 'Women shall with justice have rights similar to those exercised against them, although men have a status above women. Allah is mighty and wise.'

Surah 2 verse 221 'You shall not wed pagan women [idol worshippers] unless they embrace the faith. A believing slave girl is better than an idolatress, although she may please you. Nor shall you wed the idolators unless they embrace the faith. A believing slave is better than an idolator, although he may please you. These call you to hell fire, but Allah calls you, by His Will to Paradise and to forgiveness.'

Surah 4 verses 22 – 25 'Henceforth you shall not marry the women who were married to your fathers. That was an evil practice, indecent and abominable. You are forbidden to take in marriage your mothers, your daughters, your sisters, your paternal and maternal aunts, daughters of your brothers and sisters, your foster mothers, your foster sisters, mothers of your wives, your step daughters who are in your charge, born of the wives with whom you have lain, it is no offence for you to marry your step daughters if you have not consummated your marriage with their mothers, and the wives of your own begotten sons. Henceforth you are also forbidden to take in marriage two sisters at one and the same time, but that which is already past. Allah is forgiving and merciful [about the past]. You are also forbidden to take in marriage, married women, except captives whom you own as slaves. Such is the decree of Allah. All women other than these are lawful unto you, provided you seek them with your wealth [Mehr] in modest conduct, not in fornication. Give them their dowry for the enjoyment you have had of them as a duty; but it shall be no offence for you to make any other agreement among yourselves after you have fulfilled your duty. Allah is wise and all knowing. If any one of you cannot afford to marry a free believing woman, let him marry a slave girl who is a believer, Allah best knows your faith; you are born one of another. Marry them with the permission of their masters and give them their dowry in all justice, provided they are honourable and chaste and have not entertained other men.'

Surah 5 verse 5 'Lawful to you are the believing women and the free women from among those who were given the Scriptures before you [Jews and Christians] provided that you give them their dowries and live in honour with them, neither committing fornication nor taking them as mistresses.'

Surah 4 verses 2 – 4 'If you fear that you cannot treat orphans [girls] with fairness then you may marry other women who seem good to you: two, three or four of them. But if you fear that you cannot maintain equality among them, marry one only or any slave girls you may own. This will make it easier for you to avoid injustice. Give women their dowry as a free gift; but if they choose to make over to you a part of it, you may regard it as lawfully yours.'

Surah 4 verse 19 'Believers it is unlawful for you to inherit the women against their will or to treat them with harshness, in order that you may force them to give up a part of what you have given them, unless they be guilty of a proven crime. Treat them with kindness; for even if you do not love them, it may well be that you may dislike a thing which Allah has meant for your own good.'

Surah 4 verse 15 'And those of your women who commit illegal sexual intercourse, take the evidence of four witnesses among you against them and if they testify, confine them, [i.e. the women] to houses until death comes to them or Allah ordains for them some [other] way.'

Surah 4 verse 34 'Men have authority over women because Allah has made the one superior to the others and because they spend their wealth to maintain them. Good women are obedient. They guard in the husband's absence what Allah orders them to guard [e.g. their chastity, their husband's property] As to those women on whose part you see ill conduct, admonish them [first], [next] refuse to share their beds, and [last] beat them [lightly, if it is useful]; but if they obey you, seek not against them means [of annoyance]. Surely Allah is Ever Most High, Most Great.'

Surah 4 verse 35 'If you fear a breach between them twain [the man and his wife] appoint two arbitrators, one from his family and the other from her's; if they both wish for peace, Allah will cause their reconciliation. Indeed Allah is Ever All Knower, Well Acquainted with all things.'

Surah 4 verses 128, 129 'And if a woman fears cruelty or desertion on her husband's part, there is no sin on them both if they make terms of peace between themselves, and making peace is better. And human inner selves are swayed by greed, but if you do good and keep away from evil, verily, Allah is Well Acquainted with what you do. You will never be able to do perfect justice between wives even if it is your ardent desire, so do not incline too much [to one of them by giving her more of your time and provision, so as to leave the other] hanging [i.e. neither divorced nor married]. And if you do justice and do all that is right and fear Allah [by keeping away from all that is wrong] then Allah is Ever Oft Forgiving, Most Merciful.'

Surah 30 verse 21 'And among His Signs is that He created for you wives [spouses] from among yourselves, that you may find repose in them, and He has put between you affection and mercy. Verily in that are indeed signs for men of sound knowledge.'

All the above quotations are related to marriage, its purpose, rules and regulations and Quranic injunctions, for both husbands and wives. According to the Quran the husband has a superior position to the wife and is to be obeyed. The wife is to be taken care of by the husband and paid her Mehr with grace and treated kindly and justly. She has to protect her chastity and her husband's property as a dutiful wife. Although Quran gives permission to men to marry up to four wives, it stresses upon the fact that it is not possible to do perfect justice to all wives, hence it is better to have only one wife. If the wife has problems with her husband, the Quran prescribes mediation by relatives or some mutual understanding among both to maintain peace. If the husband does not like his wife, he has been asked to treat her kindly and try to live in peace with her, provided she is a dutiful wife. If the wife is disobedient and misbehaves, the husband can admonish her and even punish her as prescribed, but if she obeys he is asked to make up with her with good grace. On the other hand if it is proved that she has committed a crime like fornication, she is to be punished severely. Actually fornication and adultery are major sins according to the Quran and both men and women are forbidden to do it. Both are to be punished equally for the sin as is explained in Surah Noor. While all this sounds traditional and gender biased to the modern mind, it holds a lot of common sense and is very close to ground reality. This is similar to what has been taught by all previous religions too, with some variations.

The rules about incest and prohibitions of marriage are also quite similar among all religious traditions. It shows that since the beginning of human history the relationship among the two sexes has been the same, i.e. complementary, with the male being considered more important than the woman, because he provides for the family and protects it from all dangers. Even today that is the case with most marital relationships, all over the world. Both partners have their roles to perform and both have their rights in married life. In earlier religious traditions marriage was considered irrevocable, as in Hinduism and Christianity, but according to the Quran, if life together becomes impossible for a husband and wife, they can resort to divorce. Thus Islam has a provision for divorce but it is considered undesirable and has not been encouraged in any way. It is a last resort for men and women and should never be resorted to in haste or without solid reason. There are specific conditions and a prescribed procedure for divorce, and both men and women can seek it, as mentioned in the Quran. This appears to be reasonable and practical, since in modern times, all religions have accepted it as a legal, if not religious, provision. Below we will present Quranic quotations regarding divorce.

Surah 2 verses 226 – 232 'Those who take an oath not to have sexual relation with their wives must wait for four months, then if they return [change their mind in this period] verily Allah is Oft Forgiving, Most Merciful. And if they decide upon divorce, then Allah is All Hearer, All Knower. And divorced women shall wait [as regards their marriage] for three menstrual periods, and it is not lawful for them to conceal what Allah has created in their wombs, if they believe in Allah and the Last Day. And their husbands have the better right to take them back in that period, if they wish for reconciliation. And they [women] have rights [over their husbands as regards living expenses] similar to [those of their husbands] over them [as regards obedience and respect] to what is reasonable, but men have a degree [of responsibility] over them. And Allah is All Mighty, All Wise. The divorce is twice, after that either you retain her on reasonable terms or release her with kindness. And it is not lawful for you [men] to take back [from your wives] any of your Mehr, which you have given them, except when both parties fear that they would be unable to keep the limits ordained by Allah [e.g. to deal with each other on a fair basis] Then if you fear that they would not be able to keep the limits ordained by Allah, then there is no sin on either of them if she gives back [the Mehr or part of it] for her divorce[Al Khula]. These are the limits ordained by Allah, so do not transgress them. And whoever transgresses the limits ordained by Allah, then such are the wrongdoers. And if he has divorced her [the third time] then she is not lawful unto him thereafter until she has married another husband. Then if the other husband divorces her, it is no sin on both of them that they reunite, provided they feel that they can keep the limits ordained by Allah. These are the limits of Allah which He makes plain for the people who have knowledge. And when you have divorced women and they are about to fulfil the term of their prescribed period, either take them back on reasonable basis [if pronounced only twice] or set them free on reasonable basis [by pronouncing the third time]. But do not take them back to hurt them, and whoever does that, then he has wronged himself. And treat not the Verses [Laws] of Allah as a jest, but remember Allah's favours on you and that which He has sent down to you of the Book [Quran] and Al Hikmah [Prophet's Sunnah] whereby He instructs you. And fear Allah and know that Allah is All Knower of everything. And when you have divorced women and they have fulfilled the term of their prescribed period, do not prevent them from marrying their [former] husbands, if they mutually agree on reasonable basis [i.e. after two times]. This [instruction] is an admonition for him among you who believes in Allah and the Last Day. That is more virtuous and purer for you. Allah knows and you know not.'

These are the most comprehensive verses about divorce but there are some more in other Surahs too, which will be quoted later. Here it behoves us to observe that the rules of divorce appear to be as just as possible to both parties, i.e. husband and wife, considering the differences in their roles and obligations. For instance men have been admonished again and again not to take undue advantage of their position in any way. Women have been given the right to ask for divorce if the husband is unwilling out of perversity or meanness, by offering a part or whole of Mehr back to him. Relatives and others have been instructed to be just to both parties and never to obstruct reconciliation, if it is on reasonable basis. Men have been forbidden to reconcile if their aim is only to hurt the women. Finally Allah admonishes all people to treat Allah's laws with respect and not take them lightly. Allah says that all these instructions are for those who believe and fear Allah. This once again demonstrates that there is no compulsion in religion; if someone believes and does good, it is for his own benefit. But if someone does not believe and does wrong, he alone will be responsible for it.

Surah 65 verses 1 -2 'O Prophet! When you divorce women, divorce them at their Iddah [prescribed periods] and count [accurately] their Iddah [periods]. And fear Allah your Lord. And turn them not out of their [husbands'] homes nor shall they themselves leave, except in case they are guilty of some open illegal sexual intercourse. And those are the set limits of Allah. And whosoever transgresses the set limits of Allah, then indeed he has wronged himself. You [the one who divorces his wife] know not it may be that Allah will afterward bring some new thing to pass [i.e. to return her back to you if it was the first or second divorce] Then when they are about to attain their term appointed, either take them back in a good manner or part with them in a good manner. And take as witness two just persons from among you [Muslims]. And establish the testimony for Allah. That will be an admonition given to him who believes in Allah and the Last Day. And whosoever fears Allah and keeps his duty to Him, He will make a way for him to get out [of any difficulty].

Surah 65 verse 4 'And those of your women as have passed the age of monthly courses, the Iddah [prescribed period] if you have doubt [about their periods] is three months; and for those who have no courses [i.e. they are still immature] their Iddah [prescribed period] is three months likewise. And for those who are pregnant [whether they are divorced or their husbands are dead] their Iddah is until they lay down their burden; and whosoever fears Allah and keeps his duty to Him, He will make his matter easy for him.' There is no Iddah or prescribed period for those women who are virgins when they are divorced; i.e. those with whom marriage has not been consummated. This is announced in the following quotation:

> Surah 33 verse 49 'O you who believe, when you marry believing women, and then divorce them before you have sexual intercourse with them, no Iddah [prescribed period] have you to count in respect of them. So give them a present and set them free [i.e. divorce] in a handsome manner.' This 'present' is elaborated in the following verses: Surah 2 verses 236-237 'There is no blame on you if you divorce women before consummation or the fixation of their dower; but bestow on them [a suitable gift] The wealthy according to his means and the poor according to his means; - a gift of a reasonable amount is due from those who wish to do the right thing. And if you divorce them before consummation, but after the fixation of a dower for them, then the half of the dower [is due to them] unless they remit it. Or [the man's half] is remitted by him in whose hands is the marriage tie; and the remission [of the man's half] is the nearest to righteousness. And do not forget liberality between yourselves, for Allah sees well all that you do.'

Allah knows that a divorce creates problems for women and specially for children, therefore men have been asked to avoid divorce as far as possible but if it becomes necessary then they have obligations towards the women they divorce and full responsibility of their children. The following quotations are in this regard:

Surah 2 verse 233 'The mothers should suckle their children for two whole years, [that is] for those [parents] who desire to complete the term of suckling, but the father of the child shall bear the cost of the mother's food and clothing on a reasonable basis [even if she has been divorced]. No person shall have a burden laid on him greater than he can bear. No mother shall be treated unfairly on account of her child, nor father on account of his child. And on the [father's] heir is incumbent the like of that [which was incumbent on the father]. If they both decide on weaning, by mutual consent, and after due consultation, there is no sin on them. And if you decide on a foster suckling mother for your children, there is no sin on you, provided you pay [the mother] what you agreed [to give her] on reasonable basis. And fear Allah and know that Allah is All Seer of what you do.'

Surah 65 verse 6 'Lodge them [the divorced women] where you dwell, according to your means, and do not harm them so as to straiten them [that they be obliged to leave your house]. And if they are pregnant then spend on them till they lay down their burden. Then if they give suck to the children for you, give them their due payment, and let each of you accept the advice of the other in a just way. But if you make difficulties for one another, then some other woman may give suck for him [the father of the child].' These quotations related to rules of divorce and treatment of divorced women cover all important aspects of divorce. Since divorce is permissible in Islam, there is a lot of criticism of it, specially by feminists. Unfortunately, the practice of instant triple Talaq has created more space for criticism. In all the quotations given above, there is no mention of triple divorce in one sitting, hence it is clear that the Quran does not advocate it. This practice was allowed in a specific situation during the rule of Khalifa Umar. Men continue to use it as it favours them, but clearly it is very unfavourable to women, hence should not be resorted to, because all Quranic quotations admonish against exploitation or ill treatment of divorced women in any way.

After discussing marriage and divorce, now we come to the other aspects of family life. We have discussed the role and status of husbands and wives, already. Now we consider the other members of the family. Quran gives explicit commandments about treating parents with respect and kindness, even if they are non believers. There are various verses in this regard in the Quran. We shall quote only two here.

Surah 31 verses 14, 15 'And We have enjoined on man to be good and dutiful to his parents. His mother bore him in weakness and hardship, upon weakness and hardship, and his weaning is in two years – give thanks to Me and your parents. But if they both strive with you to make you join in worship with Me others, that of which you have no knowledge, then obey them not; but behave with them in the world kindly, and follow the path of him who turns to Me in repentance and in obedience. Then to Me will be your return and I shall tell you what you used to do.'

Surah 17 verses 23, 24 'And your Lord has decreed that you worship none but Him. And that you be dutiful to your parents. If one of them or both of them attain old age in your life, say not to them a word of disrespect, nor shout at them but address them in terms of honour. And lower to them the wing of submission and humility through mercy, and say: 'My Lord! Bestow on them Your Mercy as they did bring me up when I was young.'

Children are very important in a family as the main function of marriage and family is to procreate and provide legitimate and well adjusted new members to society. The Quran also enjoins parents to bring up their children well and never kill them either due to poverty or some barbaric custom steeped in ignorance, because infanticide is a sin. Female infanticide is specially mentioned as a crime which will be punished in the Hereafter. Two quotations in this regard are as follows:

> Surah 17 verse 31 'And kill not your children for fear of poverty. We shall provide for them as well as for you. Surely the killing of them is a great sin.'

Surah 81 verses 8, 9 'And when the female [infant] buried alive [as the pagan Arabs used to do] shall be questioned: For what sin was she killed?' Besides this, men have been enjoined to treat all their relatives with kindness and help them in every way. In many places men are enjoined to maintain their relations with kinsmen and not break those relations which Allah has established. There are many verses regarding the obligations towards relatives. We know that all these injunctions are very relevant in modern times and hold a lot of good sense. Today, with the advancement in science and technology, man has achieved a lot but is gradually losing the old values which determined the behaviour of his ancestors. This is true of all societies. Man has become so selfish that he does not want to help any one, be they parents or siblings or even children. We hear increasingly about ill treatment of old parents, killing of children, specially girls, commitment of murders for family property, husbands killing wives and vice versa. The above teachings of the Quran hold good for the entire humanity and should be followed by one and all. All earlier religious texts have also taught in a similar way, but their teachings have largely been forgotten.

The family decides the lineage and also property rights. There are detailed instructions about inheritance rules in the Quran, which are mainly explained in Surah Nisa. We will not go into the details of inheritance rules; suffice it to say that the Quran gives property rights to women, as daughters, sisters, wives and mothers, although their share is half that of a man. This is so because firstly she has been given a lower status and lesser responsibilities than man and secondly because she will inherit both from her father and from her husband. When a person is about to die he has been asked to prepare his will about his property. Sons and daughters are the inheritors of father's property, mainly. The widow gets a share. The parents also get a share. When poor relatives gather at the time of distribution of shares, Quran enjoins people to also give them something. If a person dies with out parents being alive and without children, then his siblings inherit his property.

There is another aspect in which family has been mentioned in the Quran. It is natural for a man to be so absorbed with his wife and children that he forgets his duty towards Allah and other human beings. Sometimes he may be miserly due to love for his family at other times he may do harm to others or may even commit a sin for the love of his family. The most common wrong he may do is to be unjust to others. For all these reasons man is admonished to be careful and not be swayed by love for his family. The following quotations express this.

Surah 8 verse 28 'And know that your possessions and your children are but a trial and that surely with Allah is a mighty reward.'

Surah 63 verse 9 'O you who believe let not your properties or your children divert you from the remembrance of Allah. And whosoever does that, then they are the losers.'

Surah 64 verse 14 'O you who believe, Verily among your wives and your children there are enemies for you [who may stop you from the obedience of Allah]; therefore beware of them! But if you pardon [them] and overlook, and forgive [their faults], then verily, Allah is Oft Forgiving, Most Merciful.'

While the head of the family has been given greater status as well as greater responsibility towards the members of the family in worldly matters, he has also been enjoined to guide his family towards the path of righteousness, thereby saving them from Allah's wrath. The following verse clarifies this.

Surah 66 verse 6 'O you who believe! Ward off yourselves and your families against a Fire [Hell] whose fuel is men and stones, over which are [appointed] stern [and] severe, who disobey not [from executing] the Commands they receive from Allah, but do that which they are commanded.' This verse shows that while every person is responsible for his actions and no one can share the burden of another, as often told in the Quran; it is the duty of parents, specially fathers to see that their children receive proper knowledge of their religious duties and are encouraged to perform them punctually. The husbands are also expected to enjoin their wives to be righteous and god fearing. This does not reduce the importance of the mother as the first teacher of the children, nor does it reduce the responsibility of a wife as an individual regarding observation of her religious duties; it only places greater responsibility on the head of the family to lead his dependents on the path of righteousness.

Thus we have covered all important aspects of marriage and family life as described in the Quran in this chapter. It is worth noting that the basic pattern and rules are not very different to those prescribed by other religious texts. Comparatively, the rules of inheritance are more favourable to women. Women have been also given more rights, like right to Mehr, right to divorce, right to maintenance while in Iddat or suckling the baby, and right to seek redress when wronged, than they were given in earlier scriptures. This is because every new religion aimed at bringing about reforms in human society. According to the Quran it has been revealed as an ultimate guide for the entire humanity and hence gives comprehensive rules and instructions about all human institutions and affairs, which are relevant in principle for all time to come.

TRANSLATIONS

1. Hilali Mohammad Taqiuddin and The Noble Quran English Translation.
2. Khan Mohammad Mohsin 2002 Darussalam Publishers Riyadh S Arabia.

7

The People of the Scripture

As mentioned earlier, the Quran says prophets were sent from time to time to different parts of the earth and some of them were given Holy Books and Scriptures while some were not. Surah 2 verse 136 'Say [O Muslims]:' We believe in Allah and that which has been sent down to us and that which has been sent down to Ibrahim [Abraham], Ismail [Ishmael], Ishaq [Isaac], Yaqub [Jacob] and to Al asbat [the offspring of the twelve sons of Jacob] and that which has been given to Musa [Moses] and Isa [Jesus] and that which has been given to the Prophets from their Lord. We make no distinction between any of them, and to Him we have submitted [in Islam]'. However, the Quran refers mostly to the three later scriptures given to three major prophets, namely The Bible, The Gospel and The Quran. The Bible was given to Moses for the Jews, the Gospel to Jesus for the people of his time, who were also Jews; but many did not believe in him and after his death his followers among the Jews called themselves the Christians and the Quran was given to the Prophet Mohammad. Both Moses and Jesus were from the children of Israel, i.e. Jacob or Yaqub in Arabic. Jacob was a prophet himself and the son of Isaac and grandson of Abraham, the great prophet and patriarch. Abraham's other son Ishmael [Ismail] was settled by him in Arabia, where he helped his father to build the Holy Ka'aba in Mecca. There were a few prophets in his line too; but the bigger prophets like Moses, David and Jesus were born in Isaac's line. Finally the Last Prophet of Allah and of His universal religion Islam, Prophet Mohammad, pbuh, was born in Ismail's line in Arabia and he was given the Holy Quran. In the Quran the Jews and the Christians have been referred to as the People of the Scripture or Ahl e Kitab and a great deal has been mentioned about them in various Surahs. In fact the major stories and incidents described in the Quran are about Abraham and his descendents, both prophets and the common people, i.e. Bani Israel. Allah praises the Faith and the righteousness of these prophets and there are Surahs dedicated to Abraham, Joseph, Jonas, Ale Imran, Maryam, and Bani Israel; while Surah Maida is mainly about Jesus and Surah Taha and other Surahs describe the life and times of Moses. General conception among people is that the Quran denounces the people of the Scripture, but this is not correct; the Quran recounts the history of the Ahle Kitab and shows how they were the Chosen people of Allah and blessed by Him in many ways. It was only when they disobeyed and transgressed from the teachings of the Scriptures and killed Allah's Messengers that they were punished. Even so there are some among them who are righteous and have been mentioned in the Quran. Allah addresses the children of Israel, or People of the Scripture, in many verses and invites them to believe in Him and His prophet Mohammad and His book, the Holy Quran, besides the Scriptures that were sent to them earlier.

Surah 2 verses 40 – 43 'O Children of Israel! Remember My Favour which I bestowed upon you, and fulfil [your obligations to] My Covenant [with you] so that I fulfil [My obligations to] your Covenant [with Me] and fear none but Me. And believe in what I have sent down [this Quran] confirming that which is with you {the Taurat [Torah] and the Injil [Gospel]} and be not the first to disbelieve therein and buy [get] not with My verses {the Taurat [Torah] and the Injil [Gospel]} a small price [i.e. getting a small price by selling My verses] and fear Me and Me alone. And mix not truth with falsehood, nor conceal the truth [i.e. Mohammad is Allah's Messenger and his qualities are written in your Scriptures, the Taurat [Torah] and the Injil [Gospel]} while you know [the truth]. And perform Assalat and give Zakat and bow down [or submit your selves with obedience to Allah] with those who bow down.' This is the first quotation about Jews and Christians in the Quran and both are addressed as children of Israel. In the following quotations Allah says that they were His chosen people:

Surah 2 verse 47 'O Children of Israel! Remember My Favour which I bestowed upon you and that I preferred you to the to the Alamin {mankind and jinn [of your time period in the past]}.

Later on in Surah Al Baqarah, Allah reminds the Jews of all His favours and blessings bestowed on them and how they disobeyed and did wrong again and again so that Allah punished them and they fell from His Grace This is given in great detail but here we will quote some verses to authenticate this.

Surah 2 verses 51- 52 'And [remember] when We appointed for Musa [Moses] forty nights, and [in his absence] you took the calf [for worship] and you were Zalimun [wrongdoers]. Then after that We forgave you so that you might be grateful.' After this many other incidents have been mentioned where Allah favoured and forgave the Jews but finally they remained unrepentant.

Surah 2 verse 74 'Then after that your hearts were hardened and became as stones or even worse in hardness.' After this many verses describe the wrong things done by Jews of later times and the Jews present in Arabia during Prophet Mohammad's time. But Allah also mentions many times that there are some believers and righteous men among the Jews with whom He is pleased. We present some quotations in this regard.

Surah 2 verse 121 'Those [who embraced Islam from Bani Israel] to whom We gave the Book [Torah, Gospel and

Quran] recite it [follow its teachings] as it should be recited, they are the ones who believe therein. And whoso disbelieve in it [Quran] those are they who are the losers.'

Surah 3 verse 33 'Allah chose Adam, Nuh [Noah] and family of Ibrahim [Abraham] and the family of Imran above the Alamin [mankind and jinn] [of their times]

Surah 3 verse 110 'And had the people of the Scripture [the Jews and the Christians] believed it would have been better for them; among them are some who have Faith, but most of them are Al fasiqun [disobedient to Allah and rebellious against Allah's Command].'

Surah 3 verse 113 'Not all of them are alike; a party of the people of the Scripture stand for the right, they recite the verses of Allah during the hours of the night, prostrating themselves in prayer.'

Surah 4 verse 162 'But those among them [Jews] who are well grounded in knowledge, and the believers, believe in what has been sent down to you [Mohammad] and what was sent down before you; and those who perform Assalat and give Zakat and believe in Allah and in the Last Day, it is they to whom We shall give a great reward.'

Surah 28 verses 52- 54 'Those to whom We gave the Scripture [Torah and Gospel] before it, they believe in it [Quran]. And when it is recited to them they say; 'we believe in it. Verily it is the truth from our Lord. Indeed even before it, we have been from those, who submit themselves to Allah in Islam, as Muslims. These will be given their reward twice over because they are patient, and repel evil with good, and spend [in charity] out of what We have provided for them.'

Surah 17 verses 107 –109 'Say: 'It is for you to believe in it or deny it. Those to whom knowledge was given before its revelation prostrate themselves when it is recited to them and say: 'Glorious is our Lord. His promise has been fulfilled.'

They fall down upon their faces, weeping; and as they listen, their humility increases.'

There are separate verses, specifically about the Christians too.

Surah 5 verse 14 'And from those who call themselves Christians We took their Covenant, but they have abandoned a good part of the message that We sent to them. So We planted amongst them enmity and hatred till the Day of Resurrection [when they discarded Allah's Book, disobeyed His Orders and transgressed beyond bounds in Allah's disobedience] and Allah will inform them what they used to do.'

Surah 5 verse 83 – 85 'And when they [who call themselves Christians] listen to what has been sent down to the Messenger [Mohammad pbuh] you see their eyes overflowing with tears because of the truth they have recognised. They say, 'Our Lord! We believe; so write us down among the witnesses. And why should we not believe in Allah and in that which has come to us of the truth [Islamic Monotheism]? And we wish that Our Lord will admit us [into Paradise on the Day of Resurrection] along with the righteous people. So because of what they said, Allah rewarded them Gardens under which rivers flow [in Paradise]. They will abide therein forever. Such is the reward of the good-doers.'

One verse in the Quran which expresses the attitude of Jews and Christians towards the Muslims and other verses which forbid Muslims from befriending them are generally discussed and debated on. They are being quoted below. Probably they are related to the specific time of the Prophet Mohammad and may apply in other times if the same conditions prevail. In the Prophet's time while the non believers of Mecca persecuted the new Muslims, many of the Jews of Arabia joined them in denouncing the Muslims and these two groups also fought battles with Muslims, while the

Christian king of Abyssinia helped them and is said to have believed in Prophet Mohammad. During the war time Muslims were asked not to side with the enemies, who ever they may be, or to befriend them in the hope that they may not be harmed, as it reflects cowardice. The following verses should be read in this context.

Surah 5 verse 82 'Verily you will find the strongest among men in enmity to the believers [Muslims] the Jews and those who are Al mushrikun, and you will find the nearest in love to the believers [Muslims] those who say; 'we are Christians'. That is because amongst them are priests and monks and they are not proud.'

Surah 3 verse 118 'O you who believe! Take not as Bitanah [advisors, protectors, helpers, friends] those outside your religion [pagans, Jews, Christians and hypocrites] since they will not fail to do their best to corrupt you. They desire to harm you severely. Hatred has already appeared from their mouths [words] but what their breasts conceal is far worse. Indeed We have made plain to you the Ayat [proof, evidence] if you understand.'

In many other verses the Prophet and his followers have been asked to deal in a just and courteous way with the people of the Scripture and treat them kindly if they have not fought against them. The Prophet [pbuh] too, always treated them with kindness. In fact it was the exemplary behaviour of Prophet Mohammad towards one and all that attracted people to him and his message. He was known to treat his acknowledged enemies too with kindness. He set an example for all to live in peace with followers of other religious traditions. Some relevant quotations are being given below.

Surah 16 verse 125 'Call men to the path of your Lord with wisdom and kindly exhortation. Reason with them in the most courteous manner. Your Lord best knows those who stray from His path and those who are rightly guided.'

Surah 29 verse 46 'And argue not with the people of the Scripture [Jews and Christians] unless it be in[a way] that is better[with good words and in good manner, inviting them to Islamic Monotheism, with His Verses], except with such of them that do wrong; and say [to them] 'We believe in that which has been revealed to us and revealed to you; our Ilah [God] and your Ilah [God] is one [i.e. Allah] and to Him we have submitted [as Muslims].'

Surah 60 verses 8-9 'Allah does not forbid you to deal justly and kindly with those who fought not against you on account of religion nor drove you out of your homes. Verily Allah loves those who deal with equity. It is only as regards those who fought against you on account of religion, and have driven you out of your homes, and helped to drive you out, that Allah forbids you to befriend them, then such are the wrongdoers [who disobey Allah].' This is a very reasonable and logical order of Allah which has been passed on His believers.

There are verses in the Quran in which Allah tells the Jews and Christians and asks Prophet Mohammad to tell them that if they believe in Allah, His Books and Prophets, and obey Him, and stop arguing without knowledge, about various matters, they will be rewarded by Him. They are to be reminded that their forefathers were Muslims [i. e. people submitting to Allah's Will] and they should follow them. Some of these verses are quoted below.

Surah 2 verses 131-132 'When his Lord said to him[Ibrahim], 'Submit [i.e. be a Muslim] !' He said, 'I have submitted myself [as a Muslim] to the Lord of the Alamin [mankind, jinn and all that exists]. And this [submission to Allah, Islam] was enjoined by Ibrahim upon his sons and by Yaqub [saying] O my sons ! Allah has chosen for you the [true] religion, then die not except in the Faith of Islam [as Muslims- Islamic Monotheism].

Surah 2 verses 139 - 140 'Say [O Mohammad to the Jews and Christians] 'Dispute you with us about Allah while He is our Lord and your Lord? And we are to be rewarded for our deeds and you for your deeds. And we are sincere to Him [in worship and obedience]. Or say you that Ibrahim, Ismail, Ishaq, Yaqub and Al asbat [the offspring of the twelve sons of Yaqub] were Jews or Christians? Say do you know better or does Allah [know better—that they were all Muslims]? And who is more unjust than he who conceals the testimony [i.e. to believe in Prophet Mohammad when he comes as is written in their Books (see verse 7:157)] he has from Allah? And Allah is not unaware of what you do.'

Surah 3 verses 65 – 67 'O people of the Scripture [Jews and Christians]! Why do you dispute about Ibrahim, while the Taurat and the Injil were not revealed till after him? Have you then no sense? Verily you are those who have disputed about that of which you have knowledge. Why do you then dispute concerning that of which you have no knowledge? It is Allah Who knows and you know not. Ibrahim was neither a Jew nor Christian, but he was a true Muslim Hanifa [Islamic Monotheism – to worship none but Allah alone]. And he was not of Al Mushrikun.' [See verse 2:105]

Surah 5 verses 65-66. 'And if only the people of the Scripture [the Jews and the Christians] had believed[in Prophet Mohammad] and warded off evil [sin, ascribing partners to Allah] and had become pious, We would have indeed expiated from them their sins and admitted them to Gardens of pleasure [in Paradise]. And if only they had acted according to the Taurat [Torah] and Injil [Gospel] and what has [now] been sent down to them from their Lord [the Quran] they would surely have gotten provision from above them and from underneath their feet. There are from among them people who are on the right course, but many of them do evil deeds.

Surah 5 verses 68, 69 'Say [O Mohammad] 'O people of the Scripture [Jews and Christians]! You have nothing [as regards guidance] till you act according to the Taurat [Torah] and Injil [Gospel] and what has [now] been sent down to you from your Lord.' Verily that which has been sent down to you [Mohammad] from your Lord increases in most of them [their] obstinate rebellion and disbelief. So be not sorrowful over the people who disbelieve. Surely those who believe [in the Oneness of Allah, in His Messenger Mohammad and all that was revealed to him from Allah] and those who are the Jews, the Sabians and the Christians- whoever believed in Allah and the Last Day, and worked righteousness, on them shall be no fear, nor shall they grieve.'

Surah 5 verse 77 'Say [O Mohammad] 'O People of the Scripture [Jews and Christians]! Exceed not the limits in your religion [by believing in something] other than the truth, and do not follow the vain desires of people who went astray before and who misled many and strayed [themselves] from the Right Path.'

Surah 13 verse 38, 39 'For every period there is a decree [from Allah]. Allah blots out what He wills and confirms [what He wills]. With Him is the Mother of the Book [Al Lauh Al Mahfuz]

These quotations show that all Books that were sent by Allah through different Messengers carried the same message therefore the people of the Scripture are being asked to believe in the teachings of all Holy Books, namely the Torah, the Gospel and the Quran, and follow them to be successful in this world and the Hereafter.

Another issue on which the Quran addresses the people of the Scripture again and again is that they know very well from the prophesies made in their Scriptures about Prophet Mohammad, that he is truly the Messenger of Allah, but still out of arrogance and rancour, they do not believe in him. It is said in the Quran that they know Prophet Mohammad as well as they know their own sons. Surah 2 verse 146 'Those to whom We gave the Scripture [Jews and Christians] recognise him [Mohammad or the Kabah at Makkah] as they recognise their sons. But verily a party of them conceal the truth while they know it –[i.e. the qualities of Mohammad which are written in Taurat and Injil].'

Surah 6 verse 20 'Those to whom We have given the Book know this as they know their own sons Those who have lost their own souls refuse therefore to believe.'

Prophet Isa [Jesus] had made a prophesy about Prophet Mohammad which is quoted in Quran as follows:

Surah 61 verse 6 'And [remember] when Isa [Jesus] son of Maryam, said 'O Children of Israel! I am the Messenger of Allah to you, confirming the Taurat {[Torah] which came} before me, and giving glad tidings of a Messenger to come after me, whose name shall be Ahmad.' But when he {Ahmad i.e. Mohammad} came to them with clear proofs, they said, 'this is plain magic.' There are more quotations from the Quran which show that the people of the Scripture knew about the coming of Prophet Mohammad from their Scriptures and their Prophets.

Surah 2 verse 76 'And when they [Jews] meet those who believe [Muslims] they say, 'we believe', but when they meet one another in private, they say, 'Shall you [Jews] tell them [Muslims] what Allah has revealed to you [Jews, about the description and the qualities of Prophet Mohammad which are written in the Taurat (Torah)], that they [Muslims] may argue with you [Jews] about before your Lord? Have you [Jews] then no understanding?'

Surah 2 verse 89 'And when there came to them [Jews] a Book [this Quran] from Allah confirming what is with them [the Taurat and the Injil] although aforetime they had invoked Allah [for coming of Mohammad] in order to gain victory over those who disbelieved, then when there came to them that which they had recognised, they disbelieved in it. So let the Curse of Allah be on the disbelievers.'

Surah 7 verse 157 'Those who follow the Messenger, the Prophet who can neither read or write [i.e. Mohammad] whom they find written about in the Taurat [Torah] (Duet XVIII 15) and the Injil [Gospel] (John XIV 16) with them; he commands them for Al Maruf [i.e. Islamic Monotheism and all that Islam ordains]; and forbids them from Al Munkar [i.e. disbelief, polytheism of all kinds and all that Islam forbids] he allows them as lawful At-tayyibat [i.e. all that is good and lawful] and prohibits them as unlawful Al-Khabaith [all that is evil and unlawful] he releases them from their heavy burdens [of Allah's Covenant with the Children of Israel] and from the fetters [bindings] that were upon them. So those who believe in him [Mohammad] honour him, help him and follow the light [Quran] which has been sent down with him; it is they who will be successful.'

The greatest sin according to the Quran is attributing partners to Allah and unfortunately the people of the Scripture, committed this sin although their Prophets had forbidden them from doing so. The Quran therefore refutes the statements made by the Jews and Christians in this regard through many verses.

Surah 5 verses 72-75 'Surely they have disbelieved who say, 'Allah is the Messiah {Isa [Jesus]}, son of Maryam [Mary].' But the Messiah said, 'O children of Israel ! Worship Allah, my Lord and your Lord' Verily whosoever sets up partners [in worship] with Allah, then Allah has forbidden Paradise to him, and the Fire will be his abode. And for the wrongdoers there are no helpers. Surely disbelievers are those who said 'Allah is the third of the three[in a Trinity]. But there is no Ilah [god] [none who has the right to be worshipped] but one Ilah [God- Allah]. And if they cease not from what they say, verily a painful torment will befall on the disbelievers among them. Will they not turn with repentance to Allah and ask his forgiveness? For Allah is Oft Forgiving, Most Merciful. The Messiah [Jesus] son of Maryam [Mary] was no more than a Messenger, many were the Messengers that passed away before him. His mother [Mary] was a Siddiqah [truthful woman]. They both used to eat food [as any other human being, while Allah does not eat]. Look how We make the Ayat[signs, proofs, lessons] clear to them; yet look how they are deluded away [from the truth].'

Surah 9 verse 30 'And the Jews say, 'Uzair [Ezra] is the son of Allah, and the Christians say; Messiah is the son of Allah.' That is their saying with their mouths, resembling the saying of those who disbelieved aforetime. Allah's curse be on them, how they are deluded from the truth!'

The Quran describes in detail the story of Maryam, daughter of Imran, right from the time of her birth till her son, Isa was born, and also describes the life of Isa the prophet, in Surah Al Imran. We will quote some important verses below.

Surah 3 verse 45 '[Remember] when the angels said; 'O Maryam! Verily Allah gives you the glad tiding of a Word ['Be!'- and he was! i.e. Isa, the son of Maryam] from Him, his name will be Al Masih 'Isa [Jesus] the son of Maryam [Mary], held in honour in this world and in the Hereafter, and will be one of those who are near to Allah.' And when Isa [Jesus] became a prophet, he preached the eternal and universal religion as follows: Surah 3 verse 50-51 'And I have come confirming that which was before me of the Taurat [Torah] and to make lawful to you part of what was forbidden to you, and I have come to you with a proof from your Lord, so fear Allah and obey me. Truly Allah is my Lord and your Lord, so worship Him [Alone]. This is a straight path.' Compare how similar is the message to that of prophet Mohammad's as quoted above [Surah 7 verse 157]. The Quran goes on to say that Isa [Jesus] is human like Adam and both were created by Allah's word, as shown in the following verses: Surah 3 verses 59-60 'Verily the likeness of Isa [Jesus] before Allah is the likeness of Adam. He created him from dust, then [He] said to him, 'Be!' and he was. [This is] the truth from your Lord so be not of those who doubt.'

The Quran also asserts in many verses that Jesus was not crucified, instead he was raised by Allah. The following verses make this clear:

Surah 4 verses 157- 158 'And because of their saying [in boast] 'We killed Messiah Isa, son of Maryam, the Messenger of Allah,' [Allah set a seal on the hearts of the Jews] –but they killed him not, nor crucified him, but it appears so to them [the resemblance of Isa was put over another man (and they killed that man)], and those who differ there in are full of doubts. They have no [certain] knowledge, they follow nothing but conjecture. For surely they killed him not [i.e. Isa, son of Maryam]. But Allah raised him [Isa] up [with his body and soul] unto Himself [and he (Isa) is in the heavens]. And Allah is Ever All Powerful, All Wise.'

Surah 19 verses 30 – 33 'Whereupon he [baby Jesus] spoke and said: 'I am the servant of Allah. He has given me the Gospel and ordained me a prophet. His blessing is upon me wherever I go, and He has commanded me to be steadfast in prayer and to give alms to the poor as long as I shall live. He has exhorted me to honour my mother and has purged me of vanity and wickedness. I was blessed on the day I was born, and blessed I shall be on the day of my death; and may peace be upon me on the day when I shall be raised to life. Such was Jesus, the son of Mary.' All the above quotations aim to rectify the falsehoods that have crept in the beliefs of the people of the Scripture.

While the Quran points out the mistakes and sins of the people of the Scripture it also gives details of their long history and says again and again how Allah made them the

Chosen people and blessed them in many ways. The Patriarch Abraham, who is the common ancestor of Jews, Christians and Muslims, has been praised in the Quran as Haneef [the most sincere believer in One God] who should be followed by all. Prophet Mohammad is told again and again to follow Prophet Abraham. Hence it is wrong to say that the Quran only finds fault with the Jews and Christians. It also praises those among them who are good and obey Allah; it enjoins them to follow the teachings of their prophets and also of Prophet Mohammad [which are similar to those of earlier prophets] and thus regain Allah's favour.

TRANSLATIONS

1. Hilali Taqiuddin and Mohsin Khan [2002] The Noble Quran English Translation Darussalam Publishers Saudi Arabia
2. Abdullah Yusuf Ali [2007 edition] The Holy Quran English Translation Adam Publishers

8

The Meaning of Jehad

Jehad is a much maligned and highly misunderstood word. Generally its meaning is taken as a Holy war or a war to defend one's religion. There are many verses in the Quran about Jehad and many of them will be quoted in this chapter to explain its meaning and various implications. It is unfortunate that not only do non Muslims misunderstand the meaning of Jehad but many Muslims also misinterpret the word. This is the reason why terrorist activities are being termed as Jehad today. This is completely wrong. Jehad can never be equated with terrorism and shedding the blood of innocent people. Jehad literally means to persevere or strive; it may be striving to improve oneself, it may be striving to protect the downtrodden, it may be a struggle against oppression or it may be a struggle to wipe out evil and establish good. The word Jehad is used in the Quran many times in all these senses. It has also been used to order the believers to fight with the non believers who have oppressed them, ill treated them and thrown them out of their homes and worst of all tried to kill their Prophet.

Today, with a tremendous rise in terrorist activities all over the world, everyone is concerned about finding the causes for it and finding a solution. All right thinking people know that all Muslims are not terrorists nor do they support it, but since Muslims are involved increasingly in terrorist activities, a myth is being propagated that Islam exhorts its followers to jehad or Holy war and belligerent Muslims are termed as jehadis. 'Such myths get perpetrated when responsible people utter them, for instance on Sept 12th 2006, Pope Benedict XVI said at the University of Regensberg, Bavaria, that while Surah 2: 256 of the Quran mentions that there is no compulsion in religion in the later verses there is an incitement to holy war. The Quran contains no such incitement; there is no mention in it of any Holy War. The Pope forgot momentarily that a Holy War was a purely Christian concept and the call for it, i.e. the first Crusade was given in 1095 AD by Pope Urban II, who granted all those taking part in it, the soldiers of the Church, absolution from all their sins as a reward. Pope Benedict XVI did not quote any specific verse from the Quran to prove what he alluded to; so probably he mistook the Arabic word jehad for a Holy War.' [S M Murshed in TOI, April 4th 2008]. SM Murshed goes on to explain the meaning of jehad as striving or struggling for any just and righteous cause, and most emphatically not war.[1] Another article by Ranjan Roy tries to explain the causes for spread of terrorism by saying that Wahhabism is responsible for creating hatred among Muslims for the West and quotes John Esposito, of Georgetown University to explain Wahhabism: 'Wahhabism breaks one of the cardinal rules of warfare in Islam-that Muslims should not fight other Muslims. The Wahhabis or Salafis divide the world strictly into believers and non believers who must be fought.' Roy says it is this ideology that drives the Taliban and leaves no room for negotiation. [TOI Aug 2nd 2008][2] Murad Ali Baig, an author of many books on religion has also written that 'revisionists have hijacked Islam and the terrorists have moved far from the Prophet's teachings. Glorification of violence in the name of revenge and belief in revenge philosophy has plagued Islam since its earliest days. The Kharajites who believed in it, had a very narrow and extreme view of the words of the Prophet and since 18th century their followers have been the Wahabis, who gained great importance in Saudi Arabia under King Saud. This extreme brand of Islam was later to become an intrinsic part of Taliban thinking. Actually many

Wahabi ideas were a heresy to the words and actions of the Prophet whose conquest of Mecca had been achieved without shedding a drop of blood through a year long, almost Gandhian campaign of patience and moral principles. Mohammad preached peace, except in times of actual combat, and the very word Islam means absolute submission to the will of a merciful god. The Quran clearly says that killing in the name of Islam was the opposite of Jehad and had expressly forbidden an attack on anyone who had offered no offence. It was forbidden to harm or kill women and children. It was also forbidden to take hostages and to torture or kill prisoners. Even suicide is forbidden.'[3] Considering the role of Wahabi thinking in terror acts, it is difficult to understand why the West specially the USA is so friendly with Saudi Arabia which strictly follows Wahhabi ideology? Secondly, one wonders, how the Taliban or anyone else, can logically assert that some Muslims are non believers while some other are believers? In fact, no one has the right to call any one else a non believer, unless the person himself professes to be one. Thirdly how do the terrorists justify killing of innocent people, both believers and non believers, by planting bombs in congested areas. Quran explicitly forbids killing with out just cause and forbids killing of a believer under any circumstances.

In this connection a more reasonable explanation has been given by MJ Akbar; he writes, 'Peace is the avowed aim of Islam, but the Islamic faith also demands, from time to time from its followers, their blood in the defence of their faith, in a holy war defined by specific circumstances. This is Jehad. Islam has always recognised the reality of war in human affairs, and set its moral and political compass. Islam thus gives permission to fight evil valiantly but does not allow its followers to create tumult and chaos and kill innocent lives. We cannot equate terrorism with Jehad.'[4] Writing about the role of war in any religion, Rudolf Heredia writes, 'It would be difficult to find a religious community that has never resorted to violence even though its tenets provide no justification for it. No religious tradition is innocent of a history of violence, even when they do not condone it.'[5] Islam allows a fair battle in self defence or to put down evil forces who are creating tumult, but does not condone letting of innocent blood or any other form of oppression. When we give this meaning to Jehad then it becomes clear that such battles are fought in all religions. Sri Ram's fight against Ravana and David's fight against Goliath was Jehad.

In the Quran the word Jehad has been used sometimes as fighting the evil within and striving to win the approval of Allah. Surah 5 verse 35 'O ye who believe! Do your duty to Allah, seek the means of approach to Him, and strive with might and main in His cause : that ye may prosper.'

"Strive hard in the cause of Allah, as is your duty to strive" [Surah 22 verse 78] or 'And if any strive [with might and main]do so for their own souls: for Allah is free of all needs from all creation.' [Surah 29 verse 6]. It is also used in the sense of arguing with non believers or people of the Scripture regarding Islam as in the following quotations:

Surah 25 verse 52 'Therefore listen not to the unbelievers; but strive against them with the utmost strenuousness, with the [Quran].'

Surah 31 verse 15 'But if they strive to make thee join in worship with Me things of which thou hast no knowledge, obey them not.'

In many other places it has been used in the sense of a fight against evil forces who have attacked the believers. A number of conditions have been laid down for such a war against evil. First of all war is permitted only when the enemy has attacked or is persecuting; during war, fairness and justice have to be observed; if enemy inclines to peace it should be accepted; treaties should be honoured; there should be no bullying or selfish aggression. M J Akbar gives the explanation of the 'limits' as given by Abdullah Yusuf Ali, 'War is permissible in self defence and under well defined limits, which should not be transgressed in any case-women, children, old and infirm should not be molested, nor trees and crops cut down, nor peace be withheld when enemy comes to terms.'[6] This shows that even in a declared war one should be careful not to hurt innocent people leave alone targeting innocent people without any provocation, as is being done by bombers today, can never be justified. The following quotations from Quran explain everything better.

Surah 2 verses 190 - 193 'Fight in the cause of Allah those who fight you. And slay them where ever you catch them and turn them out from where they have turned you out; for tumult and oppression are worse than slaughter. But fight them not at the Sacred Mosque, unless they first fight you there; but if they fight you slay them. Such is the reward of those who suppress Faith. But if they cease, Allah is Oft Forgiving, Most Merciful. And fight them on until there is no more tumult or oppression, and there prevail Justice and faith in Allah; but if they cease let there be no hostility except to those who practice oppression.'

Surah 4 verse 75 'And how should you not fight for the cause of Allah, and for the helpless old men, women and children who say: 'Deliver us Lord, from this city of wrong doers; send forth to us a guardian from your presence; send to us one that will help us.'? Gandhiji has written that this verse motivated him to take up the cause of the Indians who were discriminated against by the British in South Africa. This shows that Allah's word can inspire anyone who has an inclination to do the right thing.

Surah 8 verse 39 'Make war on them until idolatory is no more and Allah's religion reigns supreme. If they desist Allah is cognizant of all their actions; but if they give no heed, know then that Allah will protect you. He is the noblest Helper and Protector.'

Surah 22 verse 39 'To those against whom war is made; permission is given [to fight] because they are wronged; and verily, Allah is most Powerful for their aid.'

During war, the believers have been asked to follow some instructions, which are quoted below. :

> Surah 8 verses 45 – 46 'O ye who believe! When ye meet a force, be firm and call Allah in remembrance much [and often] That ye may prosper. And obey Allah and His Messenger and fall into no disputes, lest ye lose heart and your power depart; and be patient and persevering; for Allah is with those who patiently persevere.'

Surah 8 verse 61 'If they incline to peace, make peace with them and put your trust in Allah.'

Surah 9 verses 4-5 'Those idolators who have honoured their treaties and aided none against you, with these keep faith, until their treaties have run their term. Allah loves the righteous.'

Surah 9 verse 6 'If an idolator seeks asylum with you, give him protection so that he may hear the Word of Allah, and then convey him to safety. For the idolators are ignorant men.'

Surah 9 verse 13 'Will you not fight against those who have broken their oaths and conspired to banish the Apostle? They were the first to attack you. Do you fear them? Allah is more worthy of your fear, if you are true believers.'

All these quotations show that Jehad is a fair battle in self-defence or to defend helpless people. The concept of Jehad as a fight against evil forces who have attacked believers is discussed in detail in many Surahs, like Surah Nisa and Surah Baqr, whereas the Surahs Infaal and Surah Tauba are completely dedicated to the topic. These Surahs have relevance for a particular time period to some extent while some verses are meant for all times. It is difficult to deal with every thing here but suffice it to say that the

'Cursing verses' [which curse the enemies of the Prophet who were fighting against him] and verses forbidding friendship with other groups who were the enemy are meant for that particular time. Besides this, many injunctions that have been laid down are very just and reasonable, for instance spreading rumours during wartime is condemned, suspecting believing people to be non believers in order to take away their riches has been condemned. Killing or persecuting of ordinary citizens is forbidden. Cutting of trees and spoiling farms has been forbidden, too. Prisoners are to be treated justly and those of the vanquished, who agree to pay the tax are to be left in peace to practice their own faith and be given security. All treaties have to be honoured. Prof. Habib writes that basically Islam preaches peace and the Prophet of Islam was a peace loving leader, but he was forced to fight because he was attacked. Still he conquered Mecca with minimum blood shed and set an example in forgiveness and graciousness by his large hearted behaviour after victory.[7]

Even when a fight is going on with non believers the Quran tells believers to always be just and treat kindly those who have not taken part in the war against them.

Surah 60 verses 7 –9 'It may be that Allah will establish friendship between you and those whom ye [now] hold as enemies: for Allah has power [over all things]; and Allah is Oft Forgiving, Most Merciful. Allah forbids you not, with regard to those who fight you not for [your] Faith nor drive you out of your homes, from dealing kindly and justly with them: for Allah loveth those who are just. Allah only forbids you, with regard to those who fight you for [your] Faith, and drive you out of your homes, and support [others] in driving you out, from turning to them [for friendship and protection]. It is such as turn to them [in these circumstances] that do wrong.'

Jehad is not clandestine attack or creation of tumult and anarchy, or killing of innocent people and creating an atmosphere of terror. The two are completely dissimilar. While Allah exhorts the believers to resort to Jehad, [Surah 4 verse 84] He condemns Fasad [tumult and Mischief]. While Allah promises great rewards for those who strive in the cause of Allah [Surah 4 verses 95-96] severe punishment has been prescribed for actions resulting in tumult, anarchy and riot Some quotations denouncing tumult and anarchy or mischief are given below.

Surah 2 verses 204, 205 'There is the type of man whose speech about this world's life may dazzle thee; And he calls Allah to witness about what is in his heart, yet is he the most contentious of enemies. When he turns his back, his aim everywhere is to spread mischief through the earth and destroy crops and cattle. But Allah loveth not mischief.'

Surah 5 verse 32 'On that account We ordained for the Children of Israel that if anyone slew a person—unless it be for murder or for spreading mischief in the land—it would be as if he slew the whole people. And if anyone saved a life, it would be as if he saved the life of the whole people.'

Surah 7 verses 55-56 'Call on your Lord with humility and in private: for Allah loveth not those who trespass beyond bounds. Do not mischief on the earth after it hath been set in order, but call on Him with fear and longing: for the mercy of Allah is near to those who do good.'

Surah 7 verse 85 'And do no mischief on the earth after it has been set in order; that will be best for you if you have Faith.'

Surah 5 verse 33 'The punishment of those who wage war against Allah and His Apostle, and strive with might and main for mischief through the land, is execution, or crucifixion, or the cutting off of hands and feet from opposite sides, or exile from the land. That is their disgrace in this world, and a heavy punishment is theirs in the Hereafter.'

M J Akbar has written that the terrorists of the present day are not Jehadis but Fasadis, in an article where he was commenting on the actions of the bombers who claim to be Indian Mujahideen. He writes 'The Indian Mujahideen has used Quranic verses to claim religious sanction for its heinous acts; but in the eyes of Islam terrorism is not jehad – it is a crime that deserves no mercy.' He also quoted verse 33 Surah 5 with regard to punishment of Fasaadis. The author feels, although the misguided Muslims are doing very wrong, it is difficult to say that they are waging war against Allah because these ignorant people think they are doing a service to their religion. But actually, they are disobeying the teachings of the Quran and the Prophet for which they should be condemned. They are misguided and in their mistaken zeal are actually disobeying Allah, for which they would be answerable to Him. Of course these offenders should be punished according to the rule of the land for their terrible crimes of murder and subversion. Anyway MJ Akbar has also quoted from the notes given by Abdullah Yusuf Ali, about this particular verse's translation that 'these punishments are for those who do 'mischief'', which is 'treason against the state combined with treason against Allah, as shown by overt crimes.' MJ Akbar also writes that Muslim terrorists are severely punished in Islamic countries like Saudi Arabia and Iran. He has stressed the point that creating tumult [Fasaad] cannot be equated with a legitimate war [Jehad] as is being claimed by the bombers according to press reports. Fasaad [tumult, confusion and treason against state] is worse than murder. [Surah 2 verse 191] Fasaad is forbidden and the punishment prescribed for it is severe. The Quran makes a very clear distinction between jihad, a legitimate war, and fasaad, which is illegitimate violence that spreads havoc among the innocent. Yusuf Ali explains the meaning of Jehad, in his notes on Surah 9 verse 20, [where believers are encouraged to do Jehad in Allah's cause], as follows: 'It may require fighting in Allah's cause, as a form of self sacrifice. But its [Jehad's] essence consists in a true and sincere Faith, which so fixes its gaze on Allah, that all selfish or worldly motives seem paltry and fade away... Mere brutal fighting is opposed to the whole spirit of Jehad, while the sincere scholar's pen or preacher's voice or wealthy man's contributions may be the most valuable forms of Jehad.' The Jehad e Akbar, or the greater Jehad is a struggle to cleanse oneself; war is only the Jehad e Asghar, or the lesser Jehad.' A Fasadi is one who 'spreads mischief through the land.' There is no place for terrorism in Jihad.'[8]

The Quran actually orders people to forgive and forget and show kindness to enemies. There are many verses which teach us to do good in return for evil.

Surah 13 verse 22 'Those who patiently persevere, seeking the countenance of their Lord; ——— and turn off evil with good; for such there is the final attainment of the [eternal] Home.'

Surah 23 verse 96 'Repel evil with that which is best: We are well acquainted with the things they say.'

Surah 41 verse 34 'Nor can goodness and evil be equal. Repel [Evil] with what is better : then will be between whom and thee was hatred become as it were thy friend and intimate.' Although taking revenge is natural, and Allah gives permission to take revenge in a just way, He says it is much better to forgive and forget. Quranic quotations to this effect were presented in an earlier chapter.

The happenings of the last few years have highlighted the word Jehad and many books have been written on it. In this chapter an effort has been made to explain the real meaning of Jehad with the help of Quranic quotations and to clarify that terrorist activities which kill innocent people can never be termed as Jehad.

Muslims have been provoked all over the world in recent times, specially by the Americans. They were also oppressed and persecuted in different wars; so much so that some have resorted to violence, but terrorist activities can never be justified. If need arises they should fight a fair battle as was fought by early Muslims. At the moment Muslims need to introspect and try to follow the teachings of Islam properly to redeem their good name and not bring a bad name to Islam. They have to be united in their efforts to improve their lot in this world and the Hereafter. A truly good Muslim will receive Allah's help in facing challenges and fighting evil. In the words of the Prophet Mohammad, the greater Jehad is to struggle to cleanse the impurity within. Today Muslims have to undertake this greater Jehad on a priority basis.

TRANSLATIONS

Abdullah Yusuf Ali The Holy Quran English Translation Adam Publications.

NJ Dawood The Koran A Translation Allen Lane.

References

1. Murshed TOI 'Islam Misunderstood' 14.4.2008.
2. Roy Ranjan TOI Aug. 2, 2008.
3. Murad Ali Baig TOI 'Revisionists Highjack Islam' Feb. 2008.
4. MJ Akbar, The Shad of Swords, [2002] Roli Books, New Delhi.
5. Heredia R, [2006] Economic and Political Weekly, Mumbai.
6. MJ Akbar [2002] The shade of Swords, Roli Books, New Delhi.
7. Moin Shakir 1970, Khilafat to Partition.
8. MJ Akbar TOI Aug. 10th 2008.

9

The Importance of Peace and Good will in Islam

ISLAM literally means 'peace' and 'surrender'. It is very unfortunate that in modern times Islam is being equated with violence and terror. Islam denounces violence, tumult and terror in no uncertain terms, quite often in the Quran. As described in detail in the previous chapter, Jehad does not mean only fighting; it is only a permission to defend one's self and one's faith in the face of oppression and aggression. The Quran declares time and again that Allah is Just, Most Forgiving, Most Merciful and Beneficient and He loves people who try to adopt these qualities. The Quran praises those who can forgive people for abusing or harming them, who avoid arguments with ignorant people and who try to be tolerant and patient with people who are being unreasonable. Quotations from the Quran to this effect will be quoted later. Here the aim is to show how important maintenance of peace and good will is, in the Islamic world view. Since Islam is the universal religion it is only correct that this should be so, becaue all world religions teach tolerance and mutual co existance and lay stress on peace and good will.

Many authors have written in detail about the importance of peace in Islam and the role Islam can and should play in maintenance of world peace. Mohammad Zafarullah Khan writes, 'The word Islam derives from a root which means 'peace' and 'submission'. It is interpreted as meaning the attainment of peace through submission to the will of God, that is through conformity to Divine law and guidance. In the Islamic concept, Divine law includes all law governing and regulating the universe. Peace and order are deemed essential for material, moral and spiritual progress. Among the attributes of God, the Quran mentions that He is 'the Source of Peace and the Bestower of Security,' [Surah 59, verse 23]. The establishment of peace and the maintenance of security must, therefore, be the constant objective of mankind. Every pursuit and activity which has a tendency to disturb the peace is severely condemned. 'Do not promote disorder in the earth after peace has been established.' [Surah 7 verses 55-56] and 'Do not go about committing iniquity in the earth and causing disorder.' [Surah 7 verse 74; Surah 11 verse 85; Surah 29 verse 36]. Also, 'Seek not to create disorder in the earth. Verily, God loves not those who seek to create disorder.'[Surah 28 verse77]. The Muslims are commanded to work wholly for peace, [Surah 2 verse 208].'[1]

MJ Akbar has also written, often, in his books and articles on Islam and Mulims that Islam stands for peace and denounces all forms of violence and terror. Asghar Ali Engineer has also explained the meaning of Jehad in detail and written that it does not mean violence and terror; it means striving and struggling to establish the truth and justice. Far from encouraging violence Islam preaches non violence and tolerance, to the maximum limit possible. Of course it does not encourage cowardice, hence teaches one to stand up for Truth and Justice and fight for the oppressed in order to establish peace and justice. MJ Akbar rightly writes, 'Islam, as the word implies does not seek violence. Equally Islam does not permit meek surrender either. There are circumstances in which all Muslims are commanded to fight to defend their faith.'[2] But he again writes in another article that Saladin, the greatest of Muslim warriors, told his son to be chary of shedding blood, 'for blood does not sleep. I have only reached my present position by conciliation.'[3] This shows the importance of restraint and avoidance of unnecessary violence even during war. Actually the Prophet Mohammad was the ideal example of a peaceful and benevolent leader who was equally brave and courageous in war. The following Quranic quotations are relevant here.

Surah 7 verses 199, 200 : Hold to forgiveness, Command what is right; but turn away from the Ignorant. If a suggestion from Satan assail thy [mind], seek refuge with Allah; for He heareth and knoweth [All things].'

Surah 5 verse 13 'But forgive them and overlook[their misdeeds] : for Allah loveth those who are kind.'

Surah 15 verse 85 : 'So overlook [any human faults] with gracious forgiveness.'

Surah 16 verse 125 'Invite [all] to the Way of thy Lord with wisdom and beautiful preaching and argue with them in ways that are best and most gracious; For thy Lord knoweth best who have strayed from His Path and who receive guidance.'

Surah 16 verses 126 –128 'And if ye punish let your punishment be proportionate to the wrong that has been done to you: but if ye show patience, that is indeed the best [course] for those who are patient. And do thou [Mohamad] be patient, for thy patience is but with the help from Allah; nor grieve over them: and distress not thy self because of their plots. For Allah is with those who restrain themselves and those who do good.'

Surah 37 verses 174 & 178 : 'So turn thou away from them [disbelievers] for a little while.'

Surah 42 verse 15 'Now then, for that [reason] call [them to the Faith] and stand steadfast as thou art commanded, nor follow thou their vain Desires; but say 'I believe in whatever Book Allah has sent down, and I am commanded to judge justly between you. Allah is our Lord and your Lord. For us [is the responsibility for] our deeds, and for you for your deeds. There is no contention between us and you. Allah will bring us together and to Him is [Our] final goal.'

Surah 42 verse 43 'But indeed if any show patience and forgive, that would truly be an affair of great resolution.'

Surah 43 verse 89 'But turn away from them and say 'Peace.'But soon shall they know!'

Surah 73 verse 10 'And have patience with what they say, and leave them with noble [dignity].'

Surah 74 verse 7 'But for thy Lord's [Cause] be patient and constant.'

All these quotations show that both the Prophet and his followers have been asked to exercise restraint and decency in all discussions and arguments with people of different ideology and thinking. They have to set good examples of patient and tolerant behaviour to the others. This is just what the Prophet and his followers did in the early years of the propogation of Islam. When they were persecuted by the Meccan and were ostracised, they bore all the tribulations with patience and fortitude and never broke the law or resort to violence. Peace does not only mean freedom from war but also freedom from disturbance and contention. It means quiet and satisfactory conditions to pursue one's life in a contented way. The Quran encourages man to establish these ideal conditions. For this it is essential that there is justice, mutual respect and trust, and every one has freedom of conscience. The Quran describes how prophets were sent to all parts of the earth at different times and how good believers have to believe in all these prophets and the Divine Books they were given. Thus Islam seeks to bring about reconciliation between the followers of different faiths. It holds out to them the hand of cooperation and friendship on a basis of righteousness. Hence the Quran declares often that whoever believes in God and the Last Day, and acts righteously will get his reward on the Day of Judgement. The Quran also invites people of different religious traditions to unite on the basic principle which they all profess to believe in i.e. the oneness of God. [3: 64] At the same time the Quran gives everyone the right to make his own choice and accept or reject whatever he chooses to believe in or deny. The Quran proclaims, 'There is no compulsion in matters of faith, for surely guidance has been made manifest and distinct from error.' [2: 256] This means that every person is responsible for his actions and is answerable to God. No other person is answerable for him. The Prophet himself has been told often in the Quran that he is just a messenger and admonisher; he is not expected to force people to obey Allah's message. In fact Allah says that the prophet cannot make people believe just by desiring so; only those will believe who are so inclined and whom Allah considers capable of accepting the truth.In this connection there are many Quranic quotations,which show that while the Prophet is a preacher, he is not responsible for wrongdoers. He should leave them alone if they start unnecessary arguments. It is better for the other believers too, to avoid heated arguments with ignorant disobedient people and move away from them. Quran also tells the righteous to forgive and forget and not speak ill of false gods. The idea behind all these injunctions is to avoid fights and maintain peace.

Surah 4 verse 140 'When ye hear the signs of Allah held in defiance and redicule, ye are not to sit with them unless they turn to a different theme.'

Surah 6 verse 68, 108 'Then thou seest men engaged in vain discourse about Our Signs, turn away from them unless they turn to a different theme.' & 'Revile not ye those whom they call upon besides Allah, lest they out of spite, revile Allah in their ignorance.'

Surah 25 verse 72 'Those who witness no falsehood and,

if they pass by futility, they pass by it with honourable [avoidance].'

Surah 6 verse 107 'We made thee [Mohammad] not one to watch over their doings. Nor art thou set over them to dispose of their affairs.'

Surah 7 verse 188 'Say [O Mohammad] : 'I have no power over any good or harm to myself except as Allah willeth. If I had knowledge of the unseen I should have multiplied all good and no evil should have touched me, I am but a warner. And a bringer of glad tidings to those who have faith.'

Surah 18 verse 6 'Thou wouldst only perchance, fret thy self to death, following after them in grief, if they believe not in this Message.'

Surah 26 verse 216 'Then if they disobey thee, Say : 'I am free [of responsibility] for what ye do!'

Surah 109 verses 1-3 & 6 'Say : O ye that reject Faith ! I worship not that which ye worship. Nor will ye worship that which I worship. To you be your Way and to me mine.'

The importance of Peace is expressed in many ways in the Quran. Allah says that He has taken it upon Himself to provide Peace, benevolence and mercy to His servants and He also tells the Prophet to show kindness to those who come to him. In another place Allah tells the Prophet that He has made him a kind and benevolent person hence people flock to him. The Quran proclaims again and again that Prophet Mohammad is a Blessing for the entire humanity. Peace is so important that two people are asked to bless each other with Peace and Allah's mercy when they meet. The customory greeting taught to the Believers is 'Peace be on you, and the mercy of Allah and His blessings.' Believers have been asked to send the blessings of Peace on Prophet Mohammad and also other prophets when they speak of them. Many times it is stated in the Quran that Allah calls you to Peace. In the Heavens the righteous will be greeted with blessings of Peace by the Angels. All this shows that Peace in Islam denotes the highet level of bliss and contentment. The attainment of Peace is hence the end all and be all of human life. This is similar to the concept of Moksha, or Salvation, which also means a state of bliss and freedom from all tensions. The following quotations from the Quran are relevant in this context.

Surah 2 verse 268 'The Evil One threatens you with poverty and bids you to conduct unseemly. Allah promiseth you His forgiveness and bounties and Allah careth for all and He knoweth all things.'

Surah 3 verse 159 'It is part of the Mercy of Allah that thou dost deal gently with them. Wert thou severe or harsh hearted, they would have broken away from about thee: so pass over their faults and ask for [Allah's] forgiveness for them.'

Surah 4 verse 86 'When a [courteous] greeting is offered you, meet it with a greeting still more courteous, [at least] of equal courtesy. Allah takes careful account of all things.'

Surah 6 verse 12 'Say, 'To whom belongeth all that is in heavens and on earth ?' Say, 'To Allah. He hath inscribed for Himelf [the rule of] Mercy.'

Surah 6 verse 160 'He that doeth good shall have ten times as much to his credit: he that doeth evil shall only be recompensed according to his evil. No wrong shall be done unto [any of] them.'

Surah 10 verse 10 '[This will be] their [righteous people's] prayer therein [Heaven]: 'Glory to thee, O Allah!' and 'Peace' will be their greeting therein.'

Surah 10 verse 25 'But Allah doth call to the Home of Peace : He doth guide whom He pleaseth to a Way that is straight.'

Surah 13 verse 6 'But verily thy Lord is full of forgiveness for mankind for their wrong doing.'

Surah 13 verses 23, 24 'And angels shall enter unto them from every gate [with the salutation]: 'Peace unto you for that ye persevered in patience ! Now how excellent is the final Home [Heaven]!'

Surah 14 verse 23 'But those who believe and work righteousness will be admitted to gardens beneath which river flow, - to dwell therein for aye with the leave of their Lord : Their greeting therein will be 'Peace!"

Surah 36 verse 57,58 '[Every] fruit will be there[in Heaven] for them; they shall have whatever they call for; 'Peace!' a Word [of salutation] from a Lord Most Merciful!'

Surah 26 verse 215 'And lower thy [O Mohammad] wing to the Believers who follow thee.'

Surah 28 verse 77 'Do thou good as Allah has been good to thee and seek not [occasions for] mischief in the land. For Allah loveth not those who do mischief.'

Surah 33 verse 43 'He it is Who sends Blessings on you, as do His angels, that He may bring you out from the depths of darkness into Light; and He is full of Mercy to the Believers.'

Surah 33 verse 56 'Allah and His angels send Blessings on the Prophet: O ye that believe! Send ye blessings on him, and salute him with all respect.'

Surah 50 verses 32-34 '[A voice will say] 'this is what was promised for you, for every penitent heedful one, who feared The Most Gracious Unseen, and brought a heart turned in devotion [to Him]: 'Enter ye therein in Peace and Security ; This is a Day of Eternal Life!' This shows that Peace is the ultimate achievement or reward for a believing human being. Once again we can equate it with salvation. Hence Peace is the most important goal towards which one is expected to work in his whole life, so that he can achieve salvation in the Hereafter.

While the Quran has given permision to the oppressed to fight for their rights and to defend their Faith, it has laid down many rules and regulations for this as mentioned in great detail in the previous chapter. Laying down of rules is basically meant to avoid injustice and mischief which Allah condemns categorically. Even during times of war one has to be careful about not disturbing the peace and order of a land unnecessarily. Hence it has been said in the Quran that innocent people and women and children should not be attacked, those who surrender should not be ill treated, and crops and animals should not be destroyed or killed. Some quotations in this respect are as follows:

> Surah 4 verse 90 '{fight the renegades] Except those who join a group between whom and you there is a treaty [of peace] or those who approach you with hearts restraining them from fighting you as well as fighting their own people. If Allah had pleased, He could have given them power over you and they would have fought you: there fore if they withdraw from you but fight you not, and instead send you [guarantees of] peace, then Allah hath opened no way for you [to war against them]

Surah 8 verse 61 'But if the enemy incline towards peace, do thou [also] incline towards peace and trust in Allah.'

Surah 9 verse 6 'If one amongst the Pagans ask thee for asylum, grant it to him, so that he may hear the Word of Allah and then escort him to where he can be secure : that is because they are men without knowledge.'

Surah 4 verse 94 'O ye who believe ! When ye go abroad in the cause of Allah, investigate carefully, and say not to anyone who offers you a salutation : 'Thou art none of Believer!' coveting the perishable goods of this life: with Allah are profits and spoils abundant. Even thus were ye yourselves before, till Allah conferred on you His favours: therefore carefully investigate. For Allah is well aware of all that ye do.'

These quotations show that even during wartime, believers should be kind and tolerant and never forget to be benevolent. They should not act in haste and cause destruction, but think before acting and find out all details before taking a decision. Peace is disturbed when there is injustice of any kind, exploitation of weaker sections by the rich and mighty or domination of one group over others either due to racial or any other feeling of superiority. The Quran condemns all such acts and enjoins people to be just and and treat every one equally. Peace can also get disturbed if people do not keep their word or if specifically they break any treaties or promises. The Quran also enjoins people to keep their promises, whether big or small, whether made individually or as a group. Zafarullah Khan has written in detail about all these aspects of peace and how Islam contributes to their achievement. 2 Here we will be giving the relevant quotations from the Quran.

Surah 5 verse 1 'O ye who believe! Fulfil [all] obligations.'

Surah 17 verse 34 'Fulfil [every] engagement [promise] for [every] engagement will be enquired into[on the Day of Reckoning].' There are many other quotations about the importance of keeping one's promises and Allah has ordered people to pay a fine [Kaffara] if one breaks one's promise.

Surah 8 veres 58, and 72 'If thou fearest treachery from any group, throw back their covenant to them, [so as to be] on equal terms: for Allah loveth not the treacherous.' 'As to those who believed but did not emigrate ye owe no duty of protection to them until they emigrate. But if they seek your aid in religion, it is your duty to help them, except against a people with whom ye have a treaty of mutual alliance : and remember Allah seeth all that ye do.'

Surah 9 verses 1, 4, 7 and 12 'A [declaration] of immunity from Allah and His Messenger, to those of the Pagans with hom ye have contracted mutual alliances:' '[But the treaties are] not dissolved with those Pagans with whom ye have entered into alliance and who have not subsequently faled you in aught, nor aided anyone against you. So fulfil your engagements with them to the end of their term: for Allah loveth the righteous.' 'How can there be a covenant before Allah and His Messenger, with the Pagans, except those with whom ye made a treaty near the Sacred Mosque? As long as these stand true to you, stand ye true to them: for Allah doth love the righteous.' 'But if they violate their oaths after their covenant, and attack your Faith,- fight ye the chiefs of Unfaith; for their oaths are nothing to them: that thus they may be restrained.' These verses are related to a particular incident when the unbelievers of Mecca were fighting with the Prophet and his followers, but the general injunctions hold good for all times. These include the following: if you have made a treaty you have to honour it. If the other party breaks it you can also declare it as over. If you want to break it because the other party is not keeping their word properly then you should announce it beforehand and take action only after the period you prescribe as interim period. If the other party honours the treaty you should also do so at all costs. In all these transactions one should be just and also benevolent. Prophet Mohammad set an outstanding example to humanity by following all these Quranic injunctions to the letter in his lifetime.

Surah 16 verse 91, 94–95 'Fulfil the Covenant of Allah when you have entered it, and break not your oaths after ye have confirmed them. Indeed ye have made Allah your surity: for Allah knoweth all that ye do.' 'And take not your oaths to practise deception between yourselves with the result that someone's foot may slip after it was firmly planted; and ye may have to taste the evil [consequences] of having hindered [men] from the Path of Allah, and a mighty Wrath descend on you. Nor sell the Covenant of Allah for a miserable price : for with Alah is a prize far better for you, if ye only knew.' This again shows the importance of keeping one's promises and also shows what evils may befall if you misuse your promises.

After stressing the importance of keeping one's word, we will now discuss the other steps that the Quran says should be taken to maintain peace; for instance trying to stop exploitation of the weak and domination of one group by another or any other type of injustice. With regard to domination, the example of Pharaoh and Israelites is given many times in the Quran. Pharaoh's act is condemned and Moses is sent to stop the domination. The following quote explains this :

> Surah 28 verses 4-6 'Truly Pharaoh elated himself in the land and divided its people into sections, depressing a group among them : their sons- he slew but he kept alive their females: for he was indeed an evil doer. And We wished to be gracious to those who were being depressed in the land, to make them leaders [in faith] and make them heirs to establish a firm place for them in the land, and to show Pharaoh, Haman and their hosts, what they were dreading from them.' These verses apply to all times and condemn all oppresssors as evil doers.

Allah says He is always just and will never show even a minute injustice in dealing with men. On the other hand He is extremely benevolent and forgiving. Allah enjoins people also to be just under all conditions and show benevolence whenever possible. Many verses of the Quran express this.

Surah 4 verse 40 'Allah is never unjust in the least degree : if there is any good done He doubleth it and giveth from His own Presence a great reward.'

Surah 17 verse 71 'On the Day We call together all human beings with their [respective] Imams : those who are given their record in the right hand will read it with pleasure and they will not be dealt with unjustly in the least.

Surah 6 verse 160 'He that doeth good shall have ten times as much to his credit : he that doeth evil, shall only be recompensed according to his evil. No wrong shall be done unto [any of] them.'

Surah 29 verse 40 'It was not Allah who wronged them: they wronged themselves.'

Surah 4 verse 135 'O ye who believe! Stand out firmly for justice, as witnesses to Allah, even as against yourselves, your parents or your kin, and whether it be [against] rich or poor for Allah can best protect both.'

Surah 5 verse 2 'And let not the hatred of some people in [once] shutting you out of the Sacred Mosque lead you to transgression [and hostility on your part]. Help ye one another in righteousness and piety, but help ye not one another in sin and rancour.'

Surah 5 verse 42 'If thou judge, judge in equity between them for Allah loveth those who judge in equity.

Surah 6 verse 152 'When ever ye speak, speak justly, even if a near relative is concerned; and fulfil the Covenant of Allah: thus doth He command you, that ye may remember.'

Surah 16 verse 126 'And if ye punish, let your punishment be proportionate to the wrong that has been done to you ; but if ye show patience, that is indeed the best [course] for those who are patient.'

Allah enjoins people to be straight forward in what they say, not spread misinformation and rumour and to carefully monitor the happenings before taking a final decision, lest they make a mistake and repent later. Saying something which you don't intend to do is condemned as it creates confusion and dissent. All this shows the importance of maintaining peace in society. Some relevant quotes are as follows.

Surah 17 verse 53 'Say to My servants that they should only say those things that are best: for Satan doth sow dissensions among them : for Satan is to man an avowed enemy.'

Surah 33 verses 70,71 'O ye who believe! Fear Allah and make your utterance straight forard. That He may make your conduct whole and sound and forgive you your sins.'

Surah 4 verse 83 'When there comes to them some matter touching [Public] safety or fear they divulge it. If they had only referred it to the Apostle, or to those charged with authority among them, the proper investigators would have tested it from them [direct].'

Surah 49 verses 6, and 9-12 'O ye who believe! If a sinner comes to you with any news, ascertain the truth lest ye harm people unwitingly, and afterwards become full of repentance for what ye have done.'

Surah 61 verses 2-3 'O ye who believe! Why say ye that which ye do not? Grievously hateful is it in the sight of Allah that ye say that which ye do not.'

Surah 73 verse 10 'And have patience [Mohammad] with what they [sinners] say, and leave them with noble [dignity].'

Peace being the avowed aim of Islam, believers have been asked to maintain peace near the Holy Kaaba, to maintain peace and not fight during Haj or during the Ramazan fasts and not to fight in the Sacred months when Allah has asked people to be most religious and not indulge in any fight or violent acts. Even in ordinary life people have been asked to desist from anger. Anger is said to be an evil and a sin. This is because anger blinds a person to such an extent that he loses his reason and acts rashly, hurts others and becomes violent and offensive. The following are quotations about controlling anger, during Haj, Roza and even under ordinary circumstances.

Surah 2 verse 183 'O ye who believe ! Fasting is prescribed to you as it was prescribed to those before you, that ye may [learn] Self-restraint.'

Surah 2 verse 191 'But fight them not at the Sacred Mosque, unless they [first] fight you there.'

Surah 2 verse 197 'For Hajj are the months well known. If anyone undertakes the duty therein, let there be no obscenity, nor wickedness, nor wrangling in the Hajj.'

Surah 2 verse 217 'They ask thee concerning fighting in the Prohibited Month. Say, 'fighting therein is a grave [offence]: But graver is it in the sight of Allah to prevent access to the path of Allah.'

Surah 3 verses 134-136 'Those who spend [freely] whether in prosperity or in adversity, who restrain anger, and pardon [all] men; for Allah loves those who do good. And those who having done something to be ashamed of, or wronged their own souls, earnestly bring Allah to mind, and ask for forgiveness for their sins, - and who can forgive sins except Allah? And are not obstinate in persisting knowingly in [the wrong] they have done. For such the reward is forgiveness from their Lord and Gardens with rivers flowing underneath.' This last quotation is about everyday life and shows the importance of controlling one's anger and negative feelings in all humility. What could be more effective than this in maintaining or restoring peace among human beings?

The importance of peace is also stressed in the Quran by enjoining people to answer evil with good and hope for Allah's reward for so doing, because Allah knows that it is not easy to answer evil with good; hence the reward. But if someone wants to take revenge he can do so, being careful not to exceed in retribution. Since this is human nature it has not been forbidden but then there is no reward after taking revenge. Either way a person would be satisfied and the other party also would be justly treated, because justice is an essential element of peace. The whole concept is made clear in the following quotation:

> Surah 41 verse 34–36 'Nor can goodness and evil be equal. Repel [evil] with what is better. Then will be

between whom and thee was hatred become as it were thy friend and intimate! And no one will be granted such goodness except those who exercise patience and self restraint, none but persons of the greatest good fortune. And if [at any time] an incitement to discord is made to thee by Satan, seek refuge in Allah. He is the One Who hears and knows all things.' In other quotations also it is said that Satan is the enemy of man and would always try to create misunderstandings among men so if there is any temptation to use harsh words or fight with others, one should always seek refuge with Allah and try to practise patience and restraint. This shows the importance of maintaining peace in everyday life, which as important as maintaining peace in world affairs and between nations.

Another important event quoted in the Quran which shows the significance of peace in Islam is the prayer of the Patriarch Abraham which he made to Allah after constructing the Holy Kaaba and leaving his son Ismail to settle down in Mecca. The prayer is as follows:

Surah 14 verses 35–37 'Remember Abraham said, 'O my Lord ! make this city one of peace and security : and preserve me and my sons from worshipping idol. O my Lord ! they have indeed led astray many among mankind.He then who follows my [ways] is of me, and he that disobeys me,- but Thou art indeed Oft-Forgiving, Most Merciful.O our Lord! I have made some of my offspring to dwell in a valley without cultivation, by Thy Sacred House; in order, O our Lord, that they may establish regular Prayer: so fill the hearts of some among men with love towards them and feed them with Fruits; so they may give thanks.'

Peace and relaxation [Sakeena] have also been mentioned in the Quran on the occasion when Allah provided solace to the prophet and his followers during the War of Badr. This was the highest favour of Allah to His followers and it finally led to their victory. The following quotations explain this better.

Surah 9 verse 26 'But Allah did pour His calm on the Messenger and on the Believers and sent down forces which ye saw not : He punished the Unbelievers : Thus doth He reward those without Faith.'

Surah 9 verse 40 'If ye help not [the Prophet], [it is no matter]: For Allah did indeed help him : when the Unbelievers forced him out : being the second of the two, the two were in the Cave, and he said to his companion: 'have no fear for Allah is with us.' Then Allah sent down his peace upon him, and strengthened him with forces which ye see not and humbled to the depths the word of the Unbelievers.'

Surah 48 verse 4 'It is He Who sent down Tranquility into the hearts of the Believers, that they may add Faith to their Faith.'

Surah 48 verse 18 'Allah's Good Pleasure was on the Believers when they swore Fealty to thee under the Tree: He knew what was in their hearts, and He sent down Tranquility to them, and He Rewarded them with a speedy Victory.'

Surah 48 verse 26 'While the Unbelievers got up in their hearts heat and cant- the heat and cant of Ignorance- Allah sent down His Tranquility to His Messenger and to the Believers, and made them stick close to the command of self restraint; and well were they entitled to it and worthy of it.'

These verses show that in the hour of need Allah helps the believers and sends Peace and Tranquility to them which enables them to face any challenges. Thus Peace and Tranquility are the highest qualities with which Allah blesses those who believe in Him, whenever they are in trouble and need His help.

In this entire chapter efforts were made to quote extensively from the Quran to show what great importance is given to maintenance of Peace and Goodwill in society at all times, in Islam. The Quran encourages people to do everything they can to resolve conflict without violence and avoid all those practices which are detremental to peace and good will. Even in times of war and conflict the Quran enjoins people to be just and merciful to the adversary and practise utmost restraint in punishing or taking revenge, when necessary. Thus Peace is the avowed aim of Islam and it has been identified as the greatest blessing of Allah.

TRANSLATION

Abdullah Yusuf Ali [2007] The Holy Quran English Translation Adam Publishers

REFERENCES

1. Khan Mohd. Zafarullah Islam—Its Meaning for Modern Man [1980] Routledge and Kegan Paul London.
2. Akbar M.J. [2002] In the Shade of Swords Roli Books.
3. Akbar M.J. 'Siege Within', Times of India 11th Jan 2009.

10

The Concept of Continuity and Change in Islam

Islam is a universal religion which is valid for all time. Hence the concept of continuity and change is integral to it. Ever since Allah created the Universe and created man as His Caliph on earth, He has sent guidance to mankind from time to time through His messengers. The message was basically the same but due to different circumstances of different regions at different times there were some variations in the teachings of different prophets, for intance while all prophets laid stress on belief in One Supreme Being, Prophet Nuh and Prophet Hud laid stress on worship of One God because their nations had started worshipping many idols {11 :50}. Hud also laid stress on being humble and tolerant because his people were very arrogant and punished their foes harshly {26: 130}. Prophet Saleh told his people to be obedient to God and not think themselves invincible because they were rich and powerful and carved houses and palace out of rocky mountains with great skill {26: 14–149}. Prophet Lot condemned the sodomy practised by his people {26: 165, 166} and Prophet Shoaib laid stress on being just and giving full measure when selling and transacting business honestly because his people were not honest in their dealings {26: 181-183}. Prophet Moses was given the Ten Commandments while Prophet Jesus taught the message of Love and Benevolence in his Sermon on the Mount. This shows that while there was a continuity in the Lord's Message there were also changes according to changing times and circumstances. The final messenger,

Prophet Mohammad brought many injunctions and commands which were relevant to his times as well as many others which would be relevant for all times because after him there was to be no other messenger from God. The final message was presented to the world in the form of the Holy Quran. The very fact that the Quran is meant to be a guidance to the entire humanity for all time, entails that its teachings should be amenable to interpretation relevant for all times and all regions. The Quran has some verses which are known as the Mohakamat or basic orders for man; these express the continuity in God's message while there are other verses which are time specific mostly about the Prophet's time or related to period of war. There are still other verses which are known as Mutashabihat, or verses with ambiguous meaning. Man has been asked to believe in the entire Quran as Word of God and try to understand it and follow the basic orders and pray for Allah's guidance to understand the other verses in the proper perspective. Many thinkers and reformers all over the world have tried to interpret various verses of the Quran to suit their times. This will be discussed in detail later.

Here we will try to explain the other aspect of change and continuity which we come across in the Quran. The Quran expreses how God's acts and creations are always the same, one would never find any change in God's ways or in the working of God's creations like the sun and the moon. Secondly the Quran also gives many instances of human behaviour and human history to show that events and behaviour continue to be the same what ever the age, for instance the unbelievers always rediculed and persicuted the Prophets and generally they were the rich people while the poor and oppressed supported him and believed in his teachings. On the other hand the Quran shows that there is change in everything in an orderly way. There are many verses which show the various stages that an unborn baby goes through in the mother's womb or the stages of life that a human being goes through. Similarly how the rain is formed and falls to the parched earth and brings it to life once again. There are verses which say that if one race or group of people become very unjust and cruel God will bring other people in their place who would be better. There are also verses which clarify that all that lives has to die, after reaching the best stage of one's life one goes back to an inferior stage. Thus a cyclic theory of change is propounded in the Quran. Closely related to this is the concept of duality. Quran tells us of good and bad, day and night, man and woman, rich and poor and many other such pairs. They are all complementary and have their own specific functions and qualities which are equally important.

God has created the Universe with a purpose and man has also been created with a purpose. The description of the creation of the Universe and man has been given in great detail in many verses and shows how everything has been planned in a perfect way by God. His creations operate in such a way that both continuity and change are maintained in an orderly way. Zafarullah Khan writes that according to the Quran, all God's attributes operate in accordance with the requirements of wisdom [71:13] and the creation of the heavens and earth has also been in accordance with the requirements of wisdom [15:85; 39:5: 46:3]. Its purpose is to aid man in achieving the object for which he has been created. This is part of the measure of God's unlimited bounty to man. The universe and the laws that govern it constantly work out under Divine direction, the consequences, beneficent or otherwise, of man's use of God's bounties [14:7;16: 12–16; 23: 78–80 and 6: 68 –70]. Man has to use his intellect to follow God's commands properly and use God's bounties judiciously, so that he achieves succes both in this life and the Hereafter. Man is responsible for his own actions and will be accountable for them on the Day of Judgement. (Khan Z. 'Islam'-1980).

The concept of continuity and change in the working of God's creations like the sun, the moon, the wind and the rain as well as in the birth and life cycle of man, His best creation is expressed in the following verses.

Surah 6 verses 96, 97 'He it is that cleaveth the daybreak [from the dark]: He makes the night for rest and tranquility, and the sun and moon for reckoning [of time]: such is the judgement and ordering of [Him], The Exalted in Power, The Omnicient. It is He that maketh the stars [as beacons] for you, that ye may guide yourselves with their help, through the dark paces of land and sea: We detail Our Signs for people who know. '

Surah 7 verse 54 'our Guardian Lord is Allah Who created the heavens and the earth in six Days and is firmly established on the Throne [of authority] : He draweth the night as a veil over the day, each seeking the other in rapid succession. He created the sun, the moon and the stars, [all] governed by laws under His Command. Is it not His to create and govern? Blessed be Allah, the Cherisher and the Sustainer of the Worlds!'

Surah 13 verse 4, & 15 'And in the earth are tracts [diverse though] neighbouring, and gardens of vine and fields sown with corn and palm trees –growing out of single roots or otherwise: watered with the same water, yet some of them We make more excellent than others to eat.' 'Whatever beings there are in the heavens and the earth do prostrate themselves to Allah [acknowledging subjection], with good will or inspite of themselves, so do their shadows in the mornings and evenings.'

Surah 17 verse 99 'See thou not that Allah, Who created the heavens and the earth, has power to create the like of them [anew]? Only He has decreed a term appointed, of which there is no doubt.'

Surah 21 verse 33 'It is He Who created the night and the Day, and the sun and the moon : all [the celestial bodies] swim along, each in its rounded course. '

Surah 22 verse 5 'O mankind! If ye have a doubt about the resurrection, [consider] that We created you out of dust, then out of sperm, then out of a leech like clot, then out of a morsel of flesh, partly formed and partly unformed, in order that We may manifest [Our power] to you; and We cause whom We will to rest in wombs for an appointed term, then do We bring you out as babes, then [foster you] that ye may reach your age of full strength ; and some of you are called to die, and some are sent back to the feeblest old age, so that they know nothing after having known [much].'

Surah 24 verses 43–45 'Seest thou not that Allah makes the cloud move gently, then joins them together, then makes them into a heap ?- then wilt thou see rain issue forth from their midst. And He sends down from the sky mountain masses [of clouds] wherein is hail: He strikes therewith whom He pleases and He turns it away from whom He pleases. The vivid flash of His lightning well nigh blinds the sight. It is Allah Who alternates the night and the day : verily in these things is an instructive example for those who have vision! And Allah has created every animal from water : of them there are some that creep on their bellies,some that walk on two legs; and some that walk on four. Allah creates what He wills: for verily Allah has power over all things. '

Surah 29 verse 19 'See they not how Allah originates creation, then repeats it : truly that is easy for Allah. '

Surah 30 verse 19; 22 and 23 'It is He Who brings out the living from the dead, and brings out the dead from the living, and Who gives life to the earth after it is dead : and thus shall ye be brought out [from the dead]. ' 'And among His Signs is the creation of the heavens and the earth, and the variations in your language and your colours : verily in that are Signs for those who know. And among His Signs is the sleep that ye take by night and by day, and the quest that ye [make for livelihood] out of His Bounty:verily in that are Signs for those who hearken. '

Surah 30 verses 48 –49 'It is Allah Who sends the winds, and they raise the Clouds : then does He spread them in the sky as He wills, and break them into fragments, until thou seest rain drops issue from the midst thereof : then when He has made them reach such of His servants as He wills, behold, they do rejoice !- Even though before they received [the rain] – just before this- they were dumb with despair.'

Surah 30 verse 54 'It is Allah Who created you in a state of [helpless] weakness, then gave [you] strength after weakness, then after strength gave [you] weakness and a hoary head : He creats whatever He wills, and it is He Who has all knowledge and power. '

Surah 32 verse 9 'But He fashioned him[man] in due proportion, and breathed into him of His spirit. And He gave you [the faculties of] hearing and sight and understanding: little thanks do ye give!'

Surah 36 veres 37–40 'And a Sign for them is the Night : We withdraw therefrom the Day, and behold they are plunged in darkness. And the Sun runs unto a resting place, for him: that is the decree of [Him], the Exalted in Might, the All-Knowing. And the Moon,- We have measured for her stations [to traverse] till she return like the old [and withered] lower part of a date stalk. It is not permitted to the Sun to catch up the Moon;nor can the night outstrip the day: each [just] swims along in [its own] orbit [according to Law]. '

Surah 35 verse 9 & 12 'It is Allah Who sends forth the winds so that they raise up the Clouds and We drive them to a land that is dead, and revive the earth therewith after its death: even so [will be] resurrection!' 'Nor are the two seas alike, the one palatable sweet and pleasant drink and the other salty and bitter. Yet from each [kind of water] do ye eat flesh fresh and tender and ye extract ornaments to wear, and thou seest the ships therein that plough the waves, that ye may seek [thus] of the bounty of Allah that ye may be grateful. '

Surah 39 verses 6 & 21 'He creates you in the wombs of your mothers, in stages one after another, in three veils of darkness.' 'Seest thou not that Allah sends the rain from the sky; and leads it through springs in the earth? Then He causes to grow, therewith produce of various Colours; then it withers: thou wilt see it grow yellow, then He makes it dry up and crumble away, truly in this is a Message of remembrance to men of undertanding.'

Surah 30 verse 30 'So set thou thy face truly to the religion being upright, the nature in which Allah has made mankind : no change there is in the work [wrought] by Allah: that is the true religion : but most among mankind know not.'

Surah 48 verse 23 '[Such has been] the practice of Allah already in the past: no change wilt thou find in the practice of Allah.' All these quotations and many more decribe in detail the working of the universe and all God's creations. We see how every creation be it man, the sun the moon or the star, changes according to a set pattern; how rain is formed and falls to the ground and how it puts a new life in the dead earth. Examples of rise and fall or life cycle are provided in the case of man as well the plants the phases of the moon and so on. This shows that both continuity and change are maintained in an orderly Way which has always been the same.

Another aspect of human history which displays both continuity and change is the rise and fall of different nations and races. The Quran gives details of many nations which rose to great heights, then their rulers became very arrogant and disobeyed the Word of God which resulted in their destruction due to Divine wrath. Quran also says again and again that nations rise or fall due to their own actions and are accountable for the changes in their circumstances. God rewards or punishes a nation only if it deserves it. The folowing quotations are relevant here.

Surah 5 verse 54 'O ye who believe ! if any from among you turn back from his Faith, soon will Allah produce a people whom He will love as they will love Him. - lowly with the Believers, mighty against the Rejecters, fighting in the Way of Allah, and never afraid of the reproaches of such as find fault. This is the Grace of Allah which He will bestow on whom He pleaseth; and Allah encompasseth all, and He knoweth all things.'

Surah 7 verse 100 & 137 'To those who inherit the earth in succession to its [previous] possessors, is it not a guiding [lesson] that, if We so willed, We could punish them too, for their sin, and seal up their hearts so that they could not hear ?' 'And We made a people considered weak [and of no account] inheritors of lands in both East and West, - lands whereon We sent down Our blessings. The fair promise of thy Lord was fulfilled for the Children of Israel, because they had patience and constancy, and We levelled to the ground the great work and fine buildings which Pharaoh and his people erected [with such pride]. '

Surah 9 verses 69–70 'As in the case of those before you : they were mightier than you in power and more flourishing in wealth and children. They had their enjoyment of their portion : and ye have of yours, as did those before you : and ye indulge in idle talk as they did. They! – Their works are fruitless in this world and the Hereafter, and they are the losers. Hath not the story reached them of those before them?- The people of Noah and 'Ad and Thamud ; the people of Abraham, the men of Midian and the cities overthrown. To them came their messenger with Clear Signs. It is not Allah who wrongs them but they wrong their own souls. '

Surah 6 verse 131 '[The apostle were sent] thus, for thy Lord would not detroy for their wrong doing men's habitations whilt their occupants were unwarned. '

Surah 8 verse 53 'Because Allah will never change the Grace which He hath bestowed on a People until they change what is in their [own] souls : and verily Allah is He Who heareth and Knoweth [all things]. '

Surah 9 verse 115 'And Allah will not mislead a people after He hath guided them, until He makes clear to them as to what they should avoid, for Allah hath knowledge of all things.'

Surah 13 verse 11 'Verily never will Allah change the condition of a people until they change what is in themselves, but when [once] Allah willeth a people's punishment, there can be no turning it back, nor will they find, beides Him, any to protect.'

Surah 24 verse 55 'Allah has promised to those among you who believe and work righteous deeds, that He will of a surety, grant them in the land, inheritance [of power] as He granted it to those before them, that He will establish in authority their religion- the one which He has chosen for them, and that He will change [their state], after the fear in which they [lived], to one of security and peace: 'They will worhip Me [alone] and not associate aught with Me.'

Surah 22 verse 52 'Never did We send a messenger or a prophet before thee, but, when he framed a desire, Satan threw some [vanity] into his desire, but Allah will cancel anything [vain] that Satan throws in, and Allah will confirm [and establish] His signs: for Allah is full of knowledge and wisdom.' These verses show that change has been taking place in the conditions of mankind and one people have been replaced by another due to their disobedience; then if those who were put in their place continued to be good they prospered but if they too disobeyed they were also punished and replaced. In this cycle the Way of Allah has remained the same. Similarly many prophets were sent to different people with slight variations in Allah's Message, but all were generally refuted by the rich of the land while the oppresed masses followed them. When the rich and arrogant crossed limits of decent behaviour Allah punished them and saved the prophet and his followers. This punishing of the wrongdoers and saving of the believers has always occurred in the same way, denoting continuity and unchangeability of Allah's Way. All prophets were human and hence Satan tried to tempt them but Allah cancelled the temptation and guided His messengers on the right path. All these are instances of the repitition of events in human hitory which is an acknowledged fact leading to the propogation of the cyclic theory of change.

Relevant to the concept of change and continuity is the concept of duality in nature. Every major religion has talked about duality in nature, so does Islam. While there is good in society there is also bad; while there is happiness there is also sadness. There is also a meaning behind this; one would not know the value of good until one comes across bad in life. Another purpose of this duality is to test the human being; whether he is equally good in adversity and prosperity or becomes arrogant when he prospers. Yet another purpose of duality is to complement the two elements of a pair so that they become a unit; for instance man and woman. Both men and women need each other and one is incomplete without the other. The Quran describes in detail the concept of duality in nature and how Allah has created things in pairs. The following verses exlain this.

Surah 13 verse 3 'And it is He Who spread out the earth, and set thereon mountains standing firm, and [flowing] river: and fruit of every kind He made in pairs, two and two.'

Surah 51 verse 49 'And of everything We have created pairs that ye may reflect.'

Surah 91 verses 1-10 'By the Sun and His glorious splendour; by the Moon as she follows him,by the Day as it shows up [the Sun's] glory, By the night as it conceals it; by the Fermament and its [wonderful] structure; by the earth and its [wide] expanse; by the Soul and the proportion and order given to it, and its inpiration as to its wrong and its right; truly he succeeds that purifies it. And he fails that corrupts it!'

Surah 92 verses 1-10 'By the Night as it conceals [the light]; by the Day as it appears in glory; by the creation of male and female; verily [the end] ye strive for are diverse. So he who gives [in charity] and fears [Allah], and [in all sincerity] testifies to the best, We will indeed make smooth for him the path to ease. But he who is a greedy miser and thinks himself self sufficient; and gives the lie to the best, We will indeed make smooth for him the Path to Misery.'

Surah 95 verses 4, 5 'We have indeed created man in the best of moulds. Then do We abase him [to be] the lowest of the low.'

These and similar verses show that there is an order in Allah's creations and every thing has been made in pairs so that each complements the other. It also shows the differences that exist among various creations of the same species like different types of fruit, different animals and so on. Among humans too there are different types of people; basically we can divide them into good and bad. There are many more instances of change and continuity in the Quran but here we have quoted some of them to clarify the concept as presented in the Quran.

Now we come to the dicussion of the concept of continuity and change as explained and adopted by the Muslims after the demise of the Prophet, because the followers of Prophet Mohammad had to adjust to changing circumtances in the absence of his personal guidance and advice. Since the Quran is a guidance for the entire humanity for all time to come, it is reasonable to assume that its teachings will have to be interpreted according to the time and space perspective. Many authors, both Muslim and non Muslim, have written about the principle of movement in Islam. Kapadia writes that Islam the religion, is a system of beliefs and practices initially revealed by Allah to Mohammad enshrined in the

Quran, supplemented by tradition i.e. Sunna, and modified through the ages in response to change in time and space. Although the Quran is the primary source of Muslim institutions, they have not remained unaffected by the changing condition in the centuries of their existance. In the absence of a clear and categorical anwer from the Quran, the Prophet's decisions were regarded as decisive. Usages and precepts of the Prophet came to be known as Sunna, and this is another source of Muslim institutions. After the prophet the four Caliphs, who were also his immediate companions, tried to follow his teachings in the best way possible and took decisions by concensus among all immediate companions of the prophet. This was known as 'ijma'. These decisions were reached in the light of the usage of al-Madina which was utilized by the prophet in dispensing justice. These deductions of the learned were considered infallible and were upheld by various traditions attributed to the prophet, 'My followers will never agree upon what is wrong,' 'It is incumbent upon you to follow the numerous body,' and 'Obey God and obey the prophet and those amongst you who have authority. ' The first four Caliphs tried to maintain the traditional simplicity of Islam, but new situations and conditions arose with the setting up of the Ummayyad Dynasty. Islam spread far and wide in a short period, to different regions with different cultures. New social and legal situations were created. New problems arose for whose solution neither the Quran nor the Sunna was found to be adequate guide. Such issues were dealt with by the administrators according to their own intellect and common sense. This judicial opinion was known as 'ray'. Thus local usages of different parts of the Muslim empire were integrated into the Muslim law; it is said that the Prophet had on one occasion accorded his recognition to 'ray', arbitrary human judgement, as a valid source of law, in the absence of guidance from Quran and Sunna.[1]

Meanwhile many changes were taking place in the Islamic society. Contact with richer cultures was influencing the Arabs. The wars of conquest brought in lots of wealth and concept of private property developed. Ruling classes adopted lavish life style. The main problem for the jurists was that Islamic principles were to be applied to new situations, new people and a new world altogether. The rigid appliction of original teachings of Islam was not possible. Therefore modifications and reinterpretations were required.[2] Kapadia writes modifications were made either by 'ray' or 'qiyas' which is reasoning by analogy. Yet another method was 'istehsaan', the procedure of accepting a new rule, which a jurist feels is more suitable for a particular people than the old one because of their particular habits or customs, in case where analogical deductions were not at all possible. The concepts of 'qiyas' and 'istehsan' were recognised by Abu Hanifa. Ash Shafii was aginst individual opinion, 'istehsan' but he broadened the principle of 'ijma'. According to him 'ijma' meant concensus of opinion among the learned Muslims. He provided a 'principle of movement' which helped to adjust the Muslim law to varying condition of space and time.[3]

MJ Akbar also writes about Islamic jurisprudence and mentions all the above elements of 'Ijma', 'Qiyas, 'Istehsan, besides 'Istislal' [public interest], 'Istidlal' [legal reasoning], 'Ijtihad' [independent judgement] and 'Urf' [custom]. These are all accepted in Shariah. A Fatwa is the decree of a recognised theologian on the Shariah. He writes 'there is enough space in Islamic juriprudence to accommodate the flux of history, but none for the imposition of another law.'[4]

Kapadia writes further that educated Muslims have come to realize that the social legislation of Islam is in need of some change, firstly because the Law that was given for the desert nomads cannot serve needs of an agricultural economy or of an industrial civilization, and secondly, the contact with Western civilization has provided a new pattern and ideal of marriage relationships [man-woman relationships]. But the principle of 'Ijtihad' reinterpretation of Quranic facts to bring social legislation into line with their present aspirations is denied to the modernists. According to the orthodox opinion, the Doctors of the four Schools [mujtahidun mutlaq] had done their best to interpret the Quran, and what was left undone was completed by their followers, mujtahidun fi- l – madhahib and mujtahidun bil fatwa. The gate of 'Ijtehad' was thus closed by the end of the eleventh century. Though 'Ijtehad' continued to be exercised after this period, it was, as is evident from Ibn-I-Taimiyya in the thirteenth century and Ibn-I- Abdul Wahab in the eighteenth century, for the reorientation of Islamic belief and practice according to Quranic injunctions and the traditions of the Prophet.[5]

Dube and Basilov write, 'This liberal principle[of movement] remained for a long time a fundamental tenet in the creed of Islam. During the fourth century hijri, the political factors and social factor involving internal schism and external challenges led the Muslim political and religious leaders to declare that the Islamic Shariah as they have envisaged it, was complete and perfect and there was no scope for 'Ijtehad' or reinterpretation. It is always difficult to abolish any tradition, specially when religion imparts sacredness and perpetuity to it. Hence, in the Muslim society, the social and political causes for this rigid and inflexible attitude have been ignored and even forgotten, and what remains is the sacredness and sanctity of every minute rule of the Shariah. This rigid attitude has created a problem: that of defining the relationship between the standards imposed by the religiou faith and the mundane forces that activate society: for Mulims all over the world.[6]

It is not as if the Muslim society has remained stagnant eversince: efforts have been on, all over the world in the last two hundred years to bring about reform through various movements. But reform has a double meaning as far as the Muslim world is concerned; one is in the direction of modernization and the other is in the direction of puritanism, i.e. an attempt to make Muslims give up all local customs and adopt a purely Islamic way of life. People tend to call the latter type of movements as revivalist movements. This again brings to the fore the idea of continuity and change in Islam in the sense that even the modernist do believe that the basic continuity in the form of basic tenets of Islam and clear orders of the Quran [Mohakamat] have to be maintained at all costs. The reform movement towards modernization is exemplified by the movement of Ataturk in Turkey and the revivalist movement is exemplified by the Islamic revolution of Iran. In India too we have both type of revolutions among Muslims. The revivalist movement started by Shah Waliullah and carried forward by his followers Syed Ahmad Barelvi and son Shah Aziz aimed at bringing Mulims back to the true spirit of Islam. It was anti British in nature and recommended jehad against them. On the other hand the 'Back to the Quran' movement of Sir Syed Ahmad Khan was to adapt Quranic teachings to present day customs in a land ruled by Christians. His movement was pro-British and aimed at modernizing Muslims, by giving them modern Western education, with the help of the British. He had to face stiff opposition from the orthodox elements in the community. Whenever liberals or modernists have tried to bring about reforms they have met with opposition of the orthodoxy. Revivalist movements are more welcome.

Kapadia writes that Allama Iqbal recognised the validity of reinterpretation of the foundational legal principles in the light of one's own experience and the changing conditions of the modern society, but he also acknowledged that liberalism would pose a threat to the integration of the community.

In this context it is interesting to note that a movement for social mobility among Indian Muslims which is studied as the process of Islamization in Sociology also brings out the concept of continuity and change in Islam. Yogendra

Singh writes in detail about the various aspects of Islamization in his book. He writes, 'We use the term Islamization to cover three types of movements in cultural status; an upward cultural and social [which during the Muslim rule also implied economic]mobility in the status of groups through conversion to Islam; secondly movements towards orthodoxy in cultural and religious matters among the converts to Islam; thirdly, adoption of some Islamic cultural values and styles of life by non-Mulims either for reasons of expediency and profit or due to the historical forces of culture contact.' Islamization was known as a revivalist movement par excellence, since it introduced orthodox customs and traditions, prevalent among high caste Muslims, among the new converts to Islam as well as the low caste Muslims. While some traditions were based on Islamic teachings, some others were of secular nature. Yogendra Singh further writes, 'Islamization in the form of religious revivalism, ditanced Muslims from the cultural ties exiting with Hinduism, and increased identity consciousness.'[7]

The modernists have employed another device to introduce reforms. They have tried to show, with the help of Quranic quotations, that some Muslim practices are against the spirit of Quranic teaching and hence must be modified. They have been succesful to some extent, specially in popularising education among Muslims, both men and women, in present day India. But obscurantism is preventing Muslims in many parts of the world from benefiting through modern knowledge and making progress. Unfortunately modern knowledge is being used for negative purposes and regressive measures are being adopted in social and cultural life. It is very wrong to say that imparting secular education to girls is unIslamic. Islam encourages men and women to acquire both religious and secular knowledge. At one time the Islamic empire had all the leading centres of learning in the world. Muslims contributed extensively to science, medicine, mathematics, arts and architecture by their learning and also acquainted the world with the classic knowledge of Greeks by their translation work. It is the fault of the Muslims that they have lost their former glory and are not making any efforts to regain it. There are many problems facing the Muslim world today and it is up to them to analyse their conditions and options and adopt the best course of action to make positive progress both in this world and in the next. It is incumbent upon the learned Muslims to try and reinterpret the teachings of the Quran as did their predecessors in earlier centuries, keeping in mind the fundamental concept of continuity and change which Islam teaches us. Proper efforts are bound to provide divine guidance to the community to follow the right path.

TRANSLATION

Abdullah Yusuf Ali

REFERENCES

1. Kapadia [1966] Marriage and Family in India Oxford University Press.
2. Shakir Moin [1970] Khilafat to Partition.
3. Kapadia K.M. [1966].
4. Akbar M.J. [2002] The Shade of Swords Roli Books.
5. Kapadia K.M. [1966].
6. Dube Basilov [Ed.] Secularisation in Multi Religious Societies 1983 Concept Publishing Co.
7. Singh Yogendra Modernization of Indian Tradition Thomson Press [India] Limited.

11

Some Common Themes in the Quran

The Quran is a message from the Creator of the Universe for the entire humanity for all times to come. It is the most comprehensive treatise ever from the Supreme Being. Therefore it contains injunctions and explanations about all the important aspects of human life and all essential elements of the Eternal Message to mankind. We have already noted how Allah has addressed all mankind again and again in the Quran. At times specifically people of the Scripture or the Muslims have been addressed. In a broad sense, all those who believe in God and surrender to His will are Muslims; so we can say that when Muslims or Believers are addressed they may belong to any community or region. In many places the entire mankind has been addressed very clearly, thus confirming that the Quran is a message and a guidance for all human beings. What is the message of the Quran? It tells people that they should believe in One God and His messengers, His Angels, His Holy Books and in the Day of Judgement. If you believe and do good you will be rewarded on the Day of Judgement, while if you do not believe and do wrong things you will be punished. This message is repeated many times to instil it in the minds of people. Besides this, many other truths about this world and the next and truths about human failings and weaknesses are also mentioned often. In this chapter we will present some of the oft repeated themes in the Quran and discuss their significance.

First of all, the Quran gives details of the creation of the Universe again and again. The creation of the Universe is given in detail in the Scriptures also. The description in the Quran is similar to it. It is said again and again that Allah created the entire Universe in six days. The details of other creations like the sun and the moon, the trees, the animals, the flowers and the food grains is also explained. The creation of man himself is described in detail many times. The following quotations are relevant:

> Surah 7 verse 54 'Your Guardian- Lord is Allah, Who created the heavens and the earth in six Days, and is firmly established on the Throne [of authority]: He draweth the night as a veil over the day, each seeking the other in rapid succession. He created the sun, the moon and the stars, [All] governed by laws under His Command. Is it not His to create and to govern? Blessed be Allah, the Cherisher and Sustainer of the Worlds!'

Surah 14 verse 32 'It is Allah Who hath created the heavens and the earth and sendeth down rain from the skies, and with it bringeth out fruits wherein to feed you; it is He Who hath made the ships subject to you, that they may sail through the sea by His Command; and the rivers [also] hath He made subject to you.'

Surah 30 verse 22 'And among His Signs is the creation of the heavens and the earth, and the variations in your languages and your colours: verily in that are Signs for those who know.'

Surah 30 verses 25-26 'And among His Signs is this, that heaven and earth stand by His Command; then when He calls you, by a single call, from the earth, behold, ye [straight away] come forth. To Him belongs every being that is in the heavens and on earth: all are devoutly obedient to Him.' Another important quotation is 41:9-12.

Surah 23 verses 12–16 'Man We did create from a quintessence [of clay]; then We placed him [as a drop of] sperm in a place of rest, firmly fixed; then We made the sperm into a clot of congealed blood; then of that clot We made a [foetus] lump; then We made out of that lump bones and clothed the bones with flesh; then We developed out of it another creature. So blessed be Allah, the Best to create! After that at length ye will die. Again on the Day of Judgement, will ye be raised up.'

Surah 16 verses 70 and 78 'It is Allah Who created you and takes your souls at death; and of you there are some who are sent back to a feeble age, so that they know nothing after having known [much]; for Allah is All-Knowing, All- Powerful.'

'It is He Who brought you forth from the wombs of your mothers when ye knew nothing; and He gave you hearing and sight and intelligence and affections [heart]; that ye may give thanks [to Allah].'

Surah 39 verse 6 'He created you [all] from a single Person; then created, of like nature, his mate; and He sent down for you eight head of cattle in pairs; He created you in the wombs of your mothers, in stages, one after another, in three veils of darkness; such is Allah, your Lord and Cherisher : to Him belongs [all] dominion. There is no god but He: then how are e turned away [from your true Lord?]'

Surah 75 verses 36 - 40 'Does man think that he will be left uncontrolled [without purpose]? Was he not a drop of sperm emitted [in lowly form]? Then did he become a leech-like clot: then did [Allah] make and fashion [him] in due proportion. And of him He made two sexes, male and female. Has not He [the same], the power to give life to the dead?'

There are many more verses devoted to the description of the universe and all that is in it. Some Surahs have greater details than others in this respect, for instance Surahs 24, 30, 35 and 40 give many examples of the Signs of Allah, on which men are asked to ponder so that they may understand the greatness of Allah and believe in Him. Many authors have taken these examples to explain that basically there is no conflict between the scientific principles and Quranic quotations about the creation of the universe because the description of sun, moon and stars roaming in their orbits, the creation of rain, the stages in the birth of human beings and the creation of all things from water are all accepted scientific facts. When we say the universe was created in six Days we have to keep in mind that Allah says one day in His eyes is like fifty thousand years in the eyes of men. So the six Days may actually mean six periods. [Surah 70 verse 4 'The angels and the Spirit ascend unto Him in a Day the measure whereof is [as] fifty thousand years.']

Allah tells the people again and again that this universe has not been created in vain. There is a specific purpose for the creation of the universe and mankind and that is to judge the human beings according to their actions after their death on the Day of Judgement, when they will be raised from the dead. Allah has sent His messengers to different groups of people from time to time to teach them what is good and what is evil. Now it is upto the men to choose between the two and be responsible for their actions. The following quotations are relevant in this context:

Surah 13 verses 9 –10 'Verily this Quran doth guide to that which is most right [or stable], and giveth the glad tidings to the Believers who work deeds of righteousness, that they shall have a magnificent reward; and to those who believe not in the Hereafter [it announceth] that We have prepared for them a Chastisement grievous [indeed].'

Surah 4 verse 40 'Allah is never unjust in the least degree: if there is any good [done] He doubleth it, and giveth from His own presence a great reward.'

Surah 7 verse 8-9 'The balance that day will be true [to a nicety]: those whose scale [of good] will be heavy, will prosper. Those whose scale will be light, will find their souls in perdition, for that they wrongfully treated Our Signs.'

Surah 14 verses19 –20 'Seest thou not that Allah created the Heavens and the Earth in Truth? If He so will, He can remove you and put in your place A new creation? Nor is that for Allah any great matter.'

Surah 15 verses 85, 86 'We created not the heavens, the earth, and all between them, but for just ends: and the hour is surely coming [when this will be manifest] So overlook [any human faults] with gracious forgiveness.'

Surah 16 verse 22 'Your God is one Allah : As to those who believe not in the Hereafter, their hearts refuse to know that they are arrogant.'

Surah 16 verse 24-25 'When it is said to them, 'What is it that your Lord has revealed?' they say, 'Tales of the ancients.' That they may bear on the Day of Judgement, their own burdens in full and also [something] of the burdens of those without knowledge, whom they misled. Alas how grievous the burdens they will bear.'

Surah 16 verse 27 'Then on the Day of Judgement, He will cover them [non believers] with shame and say, 'where are My 'partners' concerning whom ye used to dispute [with the godly]?' Those endued with knowledge will say, 'This Day indeed are the unbelievers covered with Shame and Misery.'

Surah 16 verse 29 – 31 'So enter the gates of Hell [unbelievers will be told] to dwell therein; thus evil indeed is the abode of the arrogant. To the righteous [when] it is said, 'What is that your Lord has revealed ?' they say, 'All that is good.' To those who do good, there is good in this world and the Home of the Hereafter is still better. And excellent indeed is the Home of the righteous. Gardens of eternity which they will enter: beneath them flow [pleasant] rivers : they will have therein all that they wish: thus doth Allah reward the righteous.'

Surah 21 verses 16 –18 'Not for [idle] sport did We create the heaven and the earth and all that is between! If it had been Our wish to take [just] a pastime, We should surely have taken it from the things nearest to Us, if We would do [such a thing.]! Nay! We hurl the truth against falsehood, and it knocks out its brain, and behold Falsehood doth perish! Ah! Woe be to you for the false things you ascribe [to Us].'

Surah 27 verses 89-90 'If any do good, he will have better than it. And they will be secure from terror that Day. And if any do evil, their faces will be thrown headlong into the Fire: Do ye receive a reward other than that which ye have earned by your deeds?'

Surah 29 verses 19 –21 'See they not how Allah originates creation then repeats it: truly that is easy for Allah. Say 'travel through the earth and see how Allah did originate creation: so will Allah produce a later creation: for Allah has power over all things. He punishes whom He pleases, and He grants mercy to whom He pleases, and towards Him are ye turned.'

Surah 30 verse 11 'It is Allah Who begins the creation; then repeats it; then shall ye be brought back to Him. On the day when the hour will come the guilty will be struck dumb with despair.'

Surah 30 verse 14 'On the Day when the hour will come that Day shall [all men] be sorted out.'

Related to this concept of a Day of Judgement and reward and punishment according to deeds is the concept of rising from the dead, because all the prophets who came to preach told their people that they will be raised from the dead on the Day of Judgement to be judged by Allah for the deeds they did during their life on earth. Every time the people did not believe in the prophets and made fun of them saying how can we be raised after our bodies are destroyed. This is also repeated again and again in the Quran and Allah refutes the non believers and tells them that it is easy for Him to raise them from the dead. The following quotations are relevant in this respect:

Surah 23 verse 34 – 37 '[the unbelievers said] Does he [prophet] promise that when ye die and become dust and bones, ye shall be brought forth [again]? Far, very far is that which ye are promised! There is nothing but our life in this world ! We shall die and we live! But we shall never be raised again!'

Surah 23 verse 82 'They say: 'What! when we die and become dust and bones could we really be raised up again? Such things have been promised to us and to our fathers before! They are nothing but tales of the ancients!'

Surah 25 verse 40 'And the unbelievers must have indeed passed through the town on which was rained a shower of evil: did they not then see it [with their own eyes]? But they expect not to be raised again.'

Surah 29 verse 19 'It is He who brings out the living from the dead, and brings out the dead from the living, and Who gives life to the earth after it is dead: and thus shall ye be brought out [from the dead].'

Surah 40 verse 57 'Assuredly the creation of the heavens and the earth is a greater [matter] than the creation of men : yet most men know not.'

Surah 35 verse 16 'If He so pleases He could blot you out and bring in a new Creation.'

Allah says again and again that it is easy for Him to raise people from the dead. He just has to say, 'Be done' and it will be done. Allah gives the example of rain, which He sends from the skies to enliven the dead and parched earth and it becomes green once again. In a similar way He will raise people from the dead.

Surah 16 verse 40 'For to anything which We have willed, We but say 'Be' and it is.'

Surah 16 verse 65 'And Allah sends down rain from the sky and gives therewith life to the earth after its death: verily in this is a sign for those who listen.'

Surah 25 verse 48, 49 'and We sent down pure water from the sky. That with it We may give life to a dead land, and slake the thirst of things We have created, — cattle and men in great number.'

Related to these concepts is Allah's declaration that He does not punish any nation or people unless they disobey His Word and create havoc. Even then Allah shows mercy and forgives all those who repent. Secondly for those who continue to do wrong and do not repent, He has fixed a time and will not punish them before that time. When the time comes, the person or the nation will be punished, and no one will be able to prevent it or delay it, even by a second. Many Quranic quotations describe all these ideas.

Surah 11 verses 116- 117 'If only there had been of the generations before you, men of righteousness who prohibited men from mischief in the earth except a few among them whom We saved [from harm]! But the wrongdoers pursued the enjoyment of the good things of life which were given them, and persisted in sin. Nor would thy Lord be the One to destroy the towns unjustly while their people are righteous.'

Surah 16 verse 61 'If Allah were to punish men for their wrong doing, He would not leave, on the [earth] a single living creature: but He gives them respite for a stated Term: when their Term expires, they would not be able to delay [the punishment] for a single hour, just as they would not be able to anticipate it [for a single hour].'

Surah 35 verse 45 'If Allah were to punish men according to what they deserve, He would not leave on the back of the earth a single living creature : but He gives them respite for a stated term : when their term expires, verily Allah has in His sight all His servants.'

Surah 25 verses 69 –70 "But the chastisement on the Day of Judgement will be doubled to him [sinner] and he will dwell therein in ignominy, - unless he repents, believes, and works righteous deeds, for Allah will change the evil of such persons into good, and Allah is Oft- Forgiving and Most Merciful.'

Surah 13 verse 11 'Verily never will Allah change the condition of a people until they change what is in themselves. But when once Allah willeth a people's punishment, there can be no turning it back, nor will they find besides Him, any to protect.'

Surah 26 verses 208- 209 'Never did We destroy a town but had its warners - by way of reminder; and We never are unjust.'

Surah 28 verse 59 'Nor was thy Lord the One to destroy a town until He had sent to its Centre a messenger, rehearsing to them Our Signs: nor are We going to destroy a population except when its members practise inequity.'

All the above quotations show how merciful and just Allah is and will not punish any one without ample reason. The door to forgiveness is always open for man; but there are men who are friends of Satan and exult in doing evil and do not repent; for such there is Allah's punishment. Allah says that when His punishment is sent to a town, everyone would suffer, so its advisable for people to be careful and avoid wrong deeds and also prevent others from doing them. The best way for a believer is to desist from evil and do good and also to encourage others to do good and desist from evil. But after this, if others do not listen then the believer is not responsible for others. The following quotations explain this better:

Surah 17 verse 15 - 16 'Who receiveth guidance, receiveth it for his own benefit : who goeth astray doth so to his own loss: no bearer of burdens can bear the burden of another : nor would We punish until We have sent a messenger [to give warning] When We decide to destroy a town, We command those among them who are given the good things of this life [to be obedient] but they continued to transgress; so that the word is proved true against them : then We destroy them utterly.'

Surah 8 verse 25 'And fear trial which affect the not in particular [Only] those of you who do wrong and know that Allah is strict in punishment.'

Surah 5 verse 105 'O ye who believe! Guard your own souls; If ye follow [right] guidance, no hurt can come to you from those who stray.' This shows that while it is natural that if a calamity befalls a town, every resident will suffer, the righteous people will be judged according to their deeds by Allah in the Hereafter. Allah is always just. He has decided everything of this universe according to a logical plan and His plans never change. His rules always apply in the same way to all people. This also has been mentioned quite often in the Quran. 'Thou wilt find no change in Our ways.' [Surah 17 verse 77]

Another concept, which is repeated quite often in the Quran, is about the ungrateful nature of man. The following quotations are relevant. They depict the real nature of most people.

Surah 10 verse 12 'When trouble toucheth a man, he crieth unto Us [in all postures] – lying down on his side, or sitting or standing. But when We have removed his affliction, he passeth on his way as if he had never cried to Us for the affliction that touched him ! Thus do the deeds of the transgressors seem fair in their eyes!'

Surah 11 verses 9 –10 'If We give man a taste, of mercy from Ourselves, and then withdraw it from him, Behold! He is in despair and [falls into] ingratitude, but if We give him a taste of [Our] favours after adversity hath touched him, he is sure to say, 'All evil has departed from me.' Behold he falls into exultation and pride.'

Surah 16 verses 53 –55 'And ye have no good thing but it is from Allah; and moreover, when ye are touched by distress, unto Him ye cry with groans; yet when He removes the distress from you, behold! Some of you turn to other gods to join with their Lord- to show their ingratitude for the favours We have bestowed on them!'

Surah 17 verse 83 'Yet when We bestow Our favours on man, he turns away and becomes remote on his side [instead of coming to Us] and when evil seizes him he gives himself to despair.'

Surah 30 verse 33 'When trouble touches men they cry to their Lord, turning back to Him in repentance: but when He gives them a taste of Mercy from Himself, behold some of them pay part worship to other gods besides their Lord, - to show their ingratitude for the [favours] We have bestowed on them.' The same words are repeated in verse 8 of Surah 39.

Surah 41 verses 49-50 'Man does not weary of asking for good [things] but if ill touches him, he gives up all hope [and] is lost in despair. When We give him a taste of some mercy from Us, after some adversity has touched him, he is sure to say: 'this is due to my [merit]: I think not that the Hour [of Judgement] will ever be established; but if I am brought back to my Lord, I have [much] good stored in His sight.'

These quotations are not about unbelievers alone but about those who believe in the Lord still commit the mistake of being ungrateful for His bounties, feeling proud when successful and giving credit to self and others for the success instead of praising the Lord. One has to give a serious thought to rectifying this common shortcoming found in most of us. Once we learn to give all credit to our Creator for our success, we will learn to be humble and dependent on the Lord's mercy. It is said in the New Testament too, that Blessed are the humble for they shall inherit the earth.

Allah says again and again that if He so wished He would have made all men alike following the same religion, but He has given people the choice to behave as they like hence we find people of different opinions and behaviours and every group thinks it is the best. The following quotations explain this theme.

Surah 2 verse 213 'Mankind was one single nation, and Allah sent messengers with glad tidings and warnings; and with them He sent the Book in Truth, to judge between people in matters wherein they differed; but the people of the Book, after the clear Signs came to them, did not differ among themselves, except through selfish contumacy.'

Surah 21 verse 92 'Verily this Ummah of yours is one Ummah and I am your Lord and Cherisher: therefore serve Me[and no other].'

Surah 23 verses 52 –53 'And verily this Ummah of yours is a single Ummah and I am your Lord and Cherisher : therefore fear Me [and no other]. But people have cut off their affair [of unity], between them into sects: each party rejoices in that which is with itself.'

Related to the above theme is the truth that all men are not the same. This is also an oft repeated theme in the Quran as shown by the following quotations:

Surah 11 verse 19 'Those who hinder [men] from the path of Allah and wish it to be crooked: these were they who denied the Hereafter!'

Surah 11 verses 23- 24 'But those who believe and work righteousness, and humble themselves before their Lord, - they will be Companions of the Garden, to dwell therein for aye! These two kinds [of men] may be compared to the blind and deaf, and those who can see and hear well. Are they equal when compared? Will ye not then take heed?'

Surah 30 verse 28 'He does propound to you a similitude from yourselves : do ye have partners among those whom your right hand possess to share as equals in the wealth We have bestowed on you ? Do ye fear them as ye fear each other?'

Surah 35 verses 19 –22 'The blind and the seeing are not alike, nor are the depths of Darkness and the Light, nor are the [chilly] shade and the [genial] heat of the sun.'

This comparison is made again and again in the Quran to show that people will continue to be both good and bad inspite of the teachings of various prophets because only those receive guidance who are so inclined; while those who are not inclined towards righteousness will never receive guidance. Man has been given intellect, so if he uses it for good, Allah will help him, otherwise he will be left in his ignorance. The Prophet is told many times that he cannot force people to follow the right path. They will only do so if they are so inclined. Then those who do good, will be rewarded and those who do evil will be punished. There is different treatment for different people.

Some verses which convey similar meaning are as follows :

Surah 6 vere 125 'For thy Lord knoweth best who have strayed from His Path and who receive guidance.'

Surah 10 verse 108 'Those who receive guidance do so for the good of their own souls; those who stray do so to their own loss.'

Surah 13 verse 27 'ay: 'Truly Allah leaveth, to stray whom He will, but He guideth to Himself those who turn to Him in penitence.'

Surah 14 verse 4 'So Allah leads astray those whom He pleases and guides whom He pleases.'

Surah 16 verse 37 'If thou art anxious for their guidance, yet Allah guideth not such as He leaves to stray, and there is none to help them.'

Surah 29 verse 62, 69 'Allah enlarges the sustenance [which He gives] to which ever of His servants He pleases ; and He [similarly] grants by [strict] measure [as He pleases].' and 'And those who strive in Our [Cause] – We will certainly guide them to Our Path; for verily Allah is with those who do right.'

Surah 16 verse 71 'Allah has bestowed His gifts of sustenance more freely on some of you than on others; those more favoured are not going to throw back their gifts to those whom their right hands possess, so as to be equal in that respect. Will they then deny the favours of Allah?' This quotation shows that economically and socially too people have different stasuses and they are happy with these differences because a rich man will not distribute all his wealth among the poor so that all become equal. But it is the duty of the rich to show their gratitude for Allah's favours by giving Zakat [obligatory tiths] and also Sadaqa [charity] to the needy. The Quran teaches people to be generous and forbids them to be miserly. Islam is a great advocate of social justice and hence it encourages the rich people and the State to help the needy.

Surah 16 verses 75 –76 'Allah set forth the Parable [of two men: one] a slave under the dominion of another: he has no power of any sort : and [the other] a man on whom We have bestowed goodly favours from Ourselves; and he spends thereof [freely]; privately and publicly : are the two equal? [by no means]; Praise be to Allah. But most of them know not.' 'Allah set forth [another] Parable of two men: one of them dumb with no power of any sort; a wearisome burden is he to his master, whichever way he directs him, he brings no good: is such a man equal with one who commands Justice, and is on a Straight Way?' The first parable tries to explain the difference between the Supreme Being and the different idols that people worship. While Allah is the Supreme Being the idols are just replicas of some ancestors who are dead and cannot harm or help anyone, while Allah is All Powerful.

The second parable says that a person who is on the right path and preaches justice cannot be the same as a person who is in the wrong and not in a position to decide what is just and what is not. Once again it is stressed that all people are not the same and hence they will be treated differently in the Hereafter. But there is always scope for people to improve in their life time. If they seriously seek guidance from Allah, it will be granted to them and Allah will also pardon all their previous sins if they sincerely seek forgiveness. So the Quran addresses the entire humanity to repent of their sins and turn to God and follow the right path.

There are many other oft repeated themes in the Quran and it is not possible to discuss all. In this chapter those themes have been elaborated upon which are very important and which apply to all human beings for all time.

TRANSLATIONS

Abdullah Yusuf Ali The Holy Quran English Tranlation.

12

A Short History of the Islamic Empire

Mohammad the prophet of Islam [peace be upon him] was born in August 570 AD. at Mecca, the principal town of Arabia. Mohammad was forty years old in 610 AD when the Divine Call came to him during his retreat in the cave Hira. Allah sent His angel, Gabriel, to the Prophet who conveyed Allah's message to him. He was asked to convey this message to the humanity. In the beginning very few believed in him, except those closest to him. He was highly honoured and trusted by his people but it was difficult for them to stop worshipping their numerous gods and owe allegience to the One and Only Allah. Gradually, ofcourse, the new doctrine of unity of God, the dignity and equality of man, and the lofty and noble goal of human exitsance atracted more and more people. The rich and mighty were still antagonistic and persecuted the Prophet and his followers in many ways. When the persecutions increased Allah ordered the prophet to migrate to Madina where the inhabitants were most willing to follow him. Prophet Mohammad set up the first Muslim State in Medina. The Meccans fought two major battles with the Muslims beides some smaller ones. The Muslim won the battle of Badr although their numbers and might were much less than that of the opponents. They lost the battle of Uhad mainly because they did not obey the Prophet's order during the battle, but Allah forgave them later. In 627 AD when Prophet Mohammad and his followers won the decisive battle of the Trench, Muslim supremacy was established in that area. In 630 AD, backed by a thousand followers, Prophet Mohammad made his triumphal entry into Mecca.

Realising the futility of any further opposition, the Quraish, the Prophet's chief antagonists, yielded. Prophet Mohammad showed his greatness in his hour of victory. He forgave all the enemies and the persecutors, except ten opposition leaders. Hitti [1970] writes, 'Such restraint and statesmanship have few parallels in history. In 632 AD Prophet Mohammad passed away in Medina [Peace be on him]. Before his death he had ordered his old friend and companion, Hazrat Abu Bakr to lead the prayer and had prayed with the congregation. After his death, Abu Bakr was chosen as the Caliph by consensus. During his rule the entire Arabian peninsula was brought under Islamic faith and rule. The hero of these early campaigns was young Khalid ibn-al- Walid. In a few months his brilliant generalship won the various tribes of Arabia and the penensula was united under one man for the first time in history. After the death of Abu Bakr, Hazrat Umar was elected the next Caliph. In his rule Muslim forces marched in two directions, one toward Iraq and Persia and the other toward Palestine and Syria. Muslims defeated Byzantine forces at the batle of Yarmuk, opening way to Jerusalem, in 636. The following year Jerusalem was taken. It was the only conquered city that Caliph Umar visited. He was sagacious in administration and audacious in war. He died from a knife wound inflicted by a Persian servant after ten years of his rule. The third Caliph was Hazrat Usman and he remained Caliph for twelve years. His term was riven with controversy. He compiled the official version of the Holy Quran. He was assasinated in 656 and the elders begged a reluctant Hazrat Ali to be the fourth Caliph. Under his rule civil wars became more intense. These four were known as Khulafai Rashidin. They were all from Quraish and Medina was their capital. In ten years after the Prophet's death Islam had spread far and wide. At that time the two world powers were the Byzantine or the East Roman empire and the Persian empire. The Islamic forces destroyed the Persian empire completely and stripped the Byzantine empire of its richest provinces in Asia and Africa, namely greater Syria and Egypt.[1] Both Philip K Hitti and MJ Akbar have commented on this phenomenal success of Muslim forces. Akbar writes, the success of Muslim arms was phenomenal and the beginning was astounding. The Muslims were driven by the spirit of Jehad.[2] Hitti writes, Arab historians, mostly theologians, explained these phenomenal conquests as Providential. The term they used for the conquest was Fatah, [opening {the way for Islam}]. In fact what triumphed in these early conquests was not so much Islam the religion as Islam the nation- state Mohammad founded.[3]

The rule of Hazrat Ali ended in 661 when he was murdered. There followed a period of struggle for the caliphate. This marked the end of one era and the beginning of another. The change was not only political, but also cultural and social. The new era was inaugurated by Mu 'awiyah, founder of the Umayyad dynasty in Damascus. This dynasty started to rule in 661 and ended in 750 AD when the last Caliph Marwan II was defeated by Abu Abbas, a distant relative of the Prophet. Abdal Malik the sixth successor of Mu 'awiyah was one of the great Caliphs and was able to put down all revolts. Mu 'awiyah and his successors rapidly established an efficient government for the new empire. They continued to employ the civil servants they found in the conquered lands. He and his heirs created over the next hundred years an empire larger than any in hitory, fused by good administration and leavened by intellectual pursuit; but when the Umayyads abandoned Islamic ideals culture degenerated and politics followed. MJ Akbr quotes Rafiq Zakaria as saying that, 'it was their betrayal of Islamic brotherhood, irrespective of race or language, that brought them down.'[4]

Abu al-Abbas started the Abbasid dynasty with its capital at Baghdad. It was the most celebrated and longest lived [750-1258] dynasty of the Islamic empire. Many authors have given detailed descriptions of important events during this Caliphate. Hitti writes, 'the shift from the Umayyad to an Abbasid regime was more than a dynastic change. It had geographic, ethnic socio-economic and political aspects. Iraq moved to the forefront and Syria receded to the background; the orientation was toward Persia. Gradually the Baghdad court became more Persian than the Damascus court was Syrian. In the new court a new office developed, the vizirate. The first vizir was a Persian, Barmaki.' Harun al Rashid was the greatest Caliph of the Abbasid dynasty. The Caliphate reached the zenith of its might and affluence under this fifth Caliph and his son al-Mamun. Harun is known for his munificence, his patronage of art and literature and his luxurious life style. Through the Arabian Nights, Harun's name has become a part of the heritage of the civilized world.[5] Though the arts of civilization flourished under the Abbasids, politically and militarily the dynasty was never as strong as the Umayyads had been at their height. The Abbasid Caliph made the mistake of replacing the Umayyads' independent –minded but loyal Arab officers by a sub servient and largely non Arab bureaucracy. The most enterprising Arabs, crowded out of administration, became scholars and merchants and lost their sense of allegiance to the dynasty. Harun al Rashid appointed a Turkish general to command an expedition, his son enlisted a personal body guard of Turkish mercenaries; a later Caliph brought Turks into the army. From mid 9th century most of the Caliphs were puppet of their Turkish generals and one province after another broke away from their grasp.

Meanwhile in 756 AD an Umayyad prince, Abdur Rahman escaped to Spain and inaugurated an independent regime. He called himself Amir. The Amirate founded by him was converted into a Caliphate by his seventh successor, Abd 'al Rahman III, who declared himself Caliph in 929 AD. Under Abd 'al-Rahman III and his son, al-Hakam [961-76] the Umayyad Caliphate in Spain reached its meridian The realm as extended nrthward at the expense of the few remaining Christian kinglets and outhward to include Moroccoand western Algeria. Its trade, industry and agriculture reached a point of affluence that aroused the admiration if not the envy of contemporary Europe. Thus two rival headships had developed in the world of Islam. A third rival, a dissident one, was the Fatimid Caliphate which rose in North Africa and later shifted to Cairo. It was set up by Ubaidullah al Mahdi. His successor, Al Muizz, conquered Egypt, built Cairo and started Al Azhar Mosque, the seat of the oldest university extant. This Caliphate ended in 1171 AD when the Sunni 'ite Salahuddin destroyed it and restred the Abbaid Caliph's name to the Friday congregational prayer.[6]

The Abbasid Caliphate was becoming weaker as more and more governors proclaimed themselves as Amirs or Sultan and became independent. The Turk and Persians were becoming powerful and became rulers in practical terms, while the Caliph remained a puppet in their hands. Next the Saljuks rose to power. They defeated the Byzantine emperor and gave Islam its first foothold in the 'Land of the Romans'. Thu Turks started dominating Asia Minor. The Saljuqs fought the Crusades and under them the realm of Islam spread once again. Saljuq domination lasted from 1055 AD to 1194 AD. It was challenged by Al Nasir, the first able Abbasid Caliph in centuries. But he was not successful entirely because the Turkish Shah whose aid he sought turned against him. He was also challenged by the Mongols. Chengiz Khan conquered lands right upto Georgia, though he did not attack Baghdad. His grandson, Halagu, conquered Baghdad in 1258 AD. Al Mustasim, the last Abbasid Caliph was defeated. Thus the Arab state came to an end.[7]

A rash of successor states, mostly Mongols, Turks, Mamluks, Persians etc. erupted all over the surface of the land. The Mamlukes were a dynasty of slaves. They ruled the mainland of Arabs as a military oligarchy for more than two and a half centuries. In 1261 one of their distinguished Sultans, Baybars, harboured a fugitive uncle of the last Caliph and set him up as a puppet caliph to bolster the alien Mamluke regime. The Ottoman Sultan Salim destroyed the Mamluke state in 1517 AD. He captured a prisoner of the Abbasid line who was titled al Mutawakkil. Salim claimed that he took the Caliphate from him. The Ottoman empire with Istambul as its capital became very powerful. In the Reader's Digest publication, 'Last Two Million Years, it is said as follows about the Ottoman empire, 'The Ottoman Empire which was to become the greatest of all Muslim states, in magnificence, territorial extent and duration, was founded at the end of the 13th century by Osman son of Ertughral, the leader of a band of Turks who had migrated into Asia Minor from central Asia. They displayed enormous energy in fighting the 'infidels' of the Byzantine Empire. Their contribution to the multi racial Community of Believer was in administration and war. The Turks were in principle, in a state of permanent warfare with their Christian neighbours as their lands were Darul Harb, and in 1481 they conquered the Byzantine Empire and and sacked its capital of Constantinople. They ruled all Asia Minor, Greece and the Balkans. A hundred years later they had taken over the entire remaining Arab Empire, and ruled from Adriatic sea to the Persian Gulf, as well as over much of North Africa. The Ottoman Turks saw themselves as part of a univeral Islamic empire. They were tolerant towards followers of other religions in their empire and they also occupied high offices; nor did they have any racial prejudice. As a result of this mixing of races, Islamic civilization in the Ottoman period is a harmonious whole.[8] Their rule continued till 1924 AD when it was abolished by Kamal Ataturk, a Turkish reformer.

We see that the most important institution of the Islamic empire was the Caliphate. MJ Akbar writes, 'The Caliphate was the one institution that survived the changing dynasties. What lay behind the strength of this idea? While Sunni Muslims spread across three continents, recognized more than one king at any given moment, they generally accepted only one of them as Caliph. There had to be a rationale for such a status. This was ably laid down in the sixteenth century by the Turkish ulema after the great Ottoman Sultan, Salem the First, managed to wrest that honour from Cairo. They offered five reasons in support of their claim: the right of the sword, the sanction of the ahl-uqd or council of elderss; nomination by the previous Caliph; guardianship of the Harmain, or the two holy cities; and pocession of the relics of the Prophet [hair from the Prophet's beard and his cloak, 'gifted' by the nominal Caliph in Cairo who had also 'gifted' the title to Salem]. Of these five the most relevant are the power of the sword and the custody of the Harmain. Indeed the two are related because without strength in the sword the holy cities cannot be protected. Muslims all over the world expected the Caliph to protect their holiest mosques and the routes to these mosques [for Hajj]. The monarchs of Persia did not claim the Caliphate from 1306 because they believe only a man from the Prophet's family can be the rightful Imam: twelve generations of Imams extended from Ali to Mohammad al Askari.[9]

Once the Ottoman Caliphate was abolished the institution of the Caliphate discontinued. Many attempts were made to revive the institution, but they failed. In India too, the Ali brothers started the Khilafat movement which was supported by Gandhiji, but it did not meet with success. In 1916, the Sheriff of Mecca, Husayn proclaimed himself as the Caliph because he was a descendent of the Prophet but drew little response. His descendents still rule Jordan but their present political set up is quite different from the

Caliphate.[10] The custody of the Harmain is now in the hands of the King of Saudi Arabia and the kingdom has managed the Harmain Shareef as well as the annual Hajj pilgrimage very effeciently till date.

The contributions of the Islamic Empire to world civilization has been tremendous. Different authors have given their own accounts of these contributions. Hitti writes in detail about contributions made to art, literature, science and philoophy, in different chapters. Here we will give only the major contributions to all these fields. He writes that language next to religion, constituted the major enduring contribution of Arabs-Arabs carried out translations of Greek and Sanskrit classics into their language. For some three hundred years, beginning from mid eighth century, Arabic was the vehicle for transmitting scientific, philosophical and literary thought, which was quantitatively and qualitatively superior to anything being transmitted in Latin, Hindi, Chinese or any other language. In science the main contributions of Islamic culture have been to astronomy, mathematics and treatment of diseases or medicine. Whatever knowledge the early Arabs had of these three scientific fields in which they later excelled must have been orally transmitted through folklore because pre Islamic culture was largely illiterate. The Islamic scholar al Kwarizmi specialized in astronomy and mathematics and his contributions include calculating by means of nine figures and zero, construction of astronomical instruments and the atlas of the heaven and the earth. In medicine the great physicians, al Razi and Ibn Sina have made many contributions. Arabs made equally good progress in the fields of alchemy and botony. The Muslim philosophers al Kindi, Ibn Sina, Ibn Rushd and Ibn Khaldun are world famous for their thought. Islamic art architecture and literature also was of great beauty and moment. The Arabs are known as a nation of poets. The Arabian Nights is a literary masterpiece.

Another account of the Islamic culture is as follows; 'Islamic civilization was a product of many minds and of many races. But their individual talent might easily have gone to waste had it not been for the genius of Mohammad. Every miniature, every mosue, every line of the poets is a tribute to him. The art and architecture of the Islamic world give ample evidence of the Muslim creative genius; but one of Islam's greatest contributions lay in the encouragement it gave to the spread of learning. The correspondence between learned men throughout the Arab-speaking world resulted in extensive collection and analysis of facts, renewing a process begun by the Greeks. It also led to huge advances in mathematical, medical and physical sciences, which were passed on to the Western world.'[11]

The contributions of Muslim Spain to the Western world has also been recorded by many writers. Both in Spain and in Sicily where Muslims ruled, they were never in a majority; and they showed an unparalleled spirit of tolerance and an artistic and intellectual flowering. Students from France and England came to sit at the feet of Muslim, Christian and Jewish scholars, to learn philosophy science and medicine. What makes Andalusia so important in the history of civilization is not just that life was lived nobly there but that it passed on to the Christian West the learning of both the Islamic and the classical world.[12] The best preserved of Andalusian palaces is Alhambra in Granada, which is a masterpiece of Muslim architecture. Rich silk fabrics with beautiful designs were exported from Andalusia all over the mediterranean. Thus the Islamic culture contributed heavily to all aspects of culture and civilization, in its time. But as commented by Hitti, 'If Islam at its best raised Arab-society to a new height of human progress, at its worst, it reached a low point of stagnation, while Europe started pulling itself out of the dark ages and entering a new era of enlightenment and renaissance leading to a revolution in science and industry. Attachment to the past and isolation from the Christian West severely affected the progress of the Islamic culture.'[13]

In the present day world there are various Muslim nations which are at different levels of modernization; some are highly weternized while others are quite conservative. New problems of social and political nature are cropping up and confrontation between the West and the Muslim nations is escalating. It is difficult to look at the Islamic world as a monolith and comment on it as such. Individually Muslims in different parts are making progress in almost all areas of development but as a community they are generally looked upon as educationally backward and this unfortunate condition has to be remedied as soon as possible by concerted efforts of the community. In the next chapter the advent and spread of Islam in the Indian sub continent is discussed in detail.

References

1. Rahman Zainab Unpublished Ph.D. Thesis entitled 'Muslims in the Changing Scenario- A Case Study of Dehradun' (1995).
2. Akbar MJ In the Shade of Swords (2002) Roli Books
3. Hitti Philip K Islam A Way of Life (1970) Oxford University Press.
4. Akbar MJ *ibid.*
5. Hitti Philip K *ibid.*
6. Rahman Zainab *ibid.*
7. Hitti Philip K. *ibid.*
8. Reader's Digest Publication, "Last Two Million Years" 1973.
9. Akbar MJ *ibid.*
10. Rahman Zainab *ibid.*
11. Reader's Digest Publication, "Last Two Million Years"
12. Reader's Digest
13. Hitti Philip K. *ibid.*

13

Islam in India

In the words of well known sociologist, Prof. Yogendra Singh, 'The contact of India with Islam is almost a millennium old. It started with the Arab conquest of the Sindh in the beginning of the eighth century.'[1] Singhal elaborates as follows, 'The Arabs had trade ties with India even before the advent of Islam and the first wave of Muslim conquerors originated with the Arabs. They gave Islam a foothold in India but did not press with expansion. They treated the Indian culture with utmost consideration and their invasions were not barbarous. The real history of Islam in India begins with the Turki Afghans' invasions. It was only when Turki Afghan rulers had established their political authority in North India that Islam began to make its impact on Indian society. The development of Islam in India was a process of evolution rather than of imposition.'[2]

MJ Akbar, in his book, The shade of swords, gives the details of the first Muslim victory in India as follows, 'The cause of Islam arrived in India when a Muslim army commanded by a young man, Mohammad bin Qasim, son in law of the Governor of Iraq, Al Hajjaj, during the reign of Caliph Walid, entered Sindh in 711. Sindhi pirates had plundered Arab trade ships returning from Srilanka and enslaved Muslim women and children. The Brahmin king of largely Buddhist Sindh, Dahir, shrugged off any responsibility and refused to pay reparations. In 712 Mohammad bin Qasim drove him out of his capital, Debal, but Dahir died in a more decisive battle in June, when an arrow of Greek fire felled him from his elephant. By 714 the Arab conquest of what is now the south of Pakistan was complete but, Islam, uncharacteristically, remained confined to this region for three centuries, checked by powerful Hindu monarchs to the north and the east, until there came Mahmud Ghazni, a military genius who never suffered defeat in three decades of constant war. Mahmud had no interest in ruling what he had conquered; but he kept the key to the door of India in the hands of governor in Lahore. His successors continued the policy of turning India into a treasure hunt. It was however the destruction of Somnath that made Mahmud into an archetypical Muslim 'yavana' [foreigner] into an invader-plunderer-rapist of popular mythology.'[3]

Mahmud was an exception in the sense that he only came to India as a plunderer, other Muslim conquerors settled in India, adopted Indian life style and ruled over the country for long periods till their dynasty was displaced by some other dynasty. 'India was invaded in succession by Arabs, Turks, Afghans and Moghuls. Although they professed a common religion, they differed from one another in habits, customs and temperament. Hence each government differed in its policy, its character and principles and its effect on the Indian society.'[4] The most powerful Muslim rule in India was that of the Moghuls. The Moghul dynasty was founded in 1526 by Babar. It was a very significant period in Indian history. Muslim rule had a significant impact on all aspects of Indian life and thought. Of all the Moghul kings, Akbar the Great did the most to synthesise the various sub cultures prevalent in the sub continent. He married a Hindu Princess and started a new religion, Deen e Ilahi, which of course did not gain popularity.

Moin Shakir writes that due to various reasons like, expansion of Islamic empire, contact with different cultures, accumulation of wealth and new requirements of administration, the Islamic society did not remain the ideal one that it was in the Prophet's time. So, at the time of the advent of Muslims in India, Islam was no longer in its original form Monarchy had become the order of the day. Splendour and pomp were gathering around the person on the throne. Purchasing and selling of slaves had revived after the Rashidin Caliphs. The decree of prohibition of wine was only on paper. The freedom and the independence of woman had become a myth. The spiritual notion of equality in Islam ceased to have political and economic reality. The Muslim tradition in India was dominated by the prevailing social system: the presence of hierarchy and class consciousness, superstitious and unrealistic modes of thought and absence of democracy and consciousness of rights. The Muslims were deeply religious but Islam had departed from the Arabian type. As most of the Muslims were converts from the Hindu fold, they shared with the Hindus the same passion and love for the soil. They had many things in common with the Hindus.

Prof. Mujeeb also writes, 'the structure of the Indian Muslim society has little resemblance to the democratic, classless community integrated and inspired by the belief in One God which the Indian Muslim fondly imagines it to have been. Indian Muslim society has been a very complex organism, containing within itself healthy and unhealthy tensions, and forces of growth, stability and decay.'[5]

There are many books written about the Muslim rule in India, which provide the details of different dynasties. Here we are more concerned with the synthesis that took place between the rulers and the ruled during this period. Singhal writes in detail about the influence of Islam on Indian society and vice versa. He writes, 'the impact of Muslim rule was greater on urban life than rural. Influenced by the royal court, the urban population attained a high degree of sophistication in language and literature, art and crafts, manners, dress, diet, luxuries and refinement. In the Indian villages where practically the entire Muslim population was descended from Hindu converts, the traditional Hindu outlook and social forms were retained.'[6]

A common Indian culture could however not be evolved unless and until Islam in turn was also influenced by Hindu culture. Thus we see that there have been numerous Hindu influences on the Muslim community in India. Hindu caste system affected Muslims in such a way that Indian Muslims developed a more or less similar caste system among themselves, although there is no concept of caste in Islam. Islam stresses equality of all humans. Many other customs and institutions not in keeping with Islamic teachings were also adopted by Indian Muslims, under the influence of native culture, which was an integral part of the life of new converts to Islam. Some examples given by D P Singhal are as follows: although Islam condemns priesthood, it developed among Indian Muslims. Islam is monotheistic and iconoclastic but Indian Muslims often venerate saints and their tombs. The Prophet rejected miracles but Indian Muslims tend to sanctify their heroes. Indian Muslims also show a remarkable fondness for ritual and ceremony, which is characteristic of Hindus. While one reason for this influence was the Hindu ancestory of many Indian Muslims, the other important reason was the presence of Hindu women in Muslim harems. These Hindu women in Muslim harems formed a powerful influence in working out the Indo Islamic synthesis.[7]

Moin Shakir writes that while some historians say Muslim rule in India was secular, some others say it was democratic and constitutional. But in truth it was a mixture of all these to some extent. It developed on the lines of absolute monarchy and the emperors claimed divine superiority and neither the Ministry nor the nobles could provide constitutional checks on the authority of the emperor. Any king gifted with a little political wisdom could visualise that a successful government was impossible without the consent and approval of the majority, i.e. non

Muslims. There fore it was expedient to follow a policy of non- interference in matters of faith and provide security to non- believers and their temples. Although the Muslim rule was not theocratic, the Ulema were a part of the political system and the Holy law guided all the actions of the kings. But in practice the kings followed a policy which was expedient and overruled the Ulema if their advice was not practical. Most kings were tolerant and did not force non believers to get converted to Islam. The greatness of Akbar lies in the fact that he incorporated the spirit of religious tolerance and understanding in the state policy. If Islam spread in India, it was not because of the sword of Akbar but because of the power of his Sufi mentors, mystic saints, like Khwaja Moinuddin Chishti. Sufi derives from Saf, an Arabic word meaning wool, for the only possession of these inspired men and women was a piece of coarse woollen cloth. Sufis owed allegiance only to God. Their lives were dedicated to a mystical union with Allah, inspired by such verses of the Quran as the one in which Allah says that He is closer to man than his jugular vein, and knows more about his inner thoughts than even the ego. The Sufis preached love of God and love of mankind. They formed a bridge between various religious faiths. Sufi saints said that all paths lead to the same Almighty. Harmony is the fundamental sufi tenet, and they spread the faith without creating rancour. They endorsed the absorption of local social rituals. Sharfuddin Maneri, for instance permitted Muslim women to wear Sindoor, the red vermillion powder that is a mark of marriage.

'The first Sufi to reach India was Mansoor al Hallaj and travelled through Sind and Punjab and became the ultimate symbol of love in popular poetry of the region. However the true impact of Sufism began with Khwaja Muinuddin Chishti who settled in Ajmer. He continues to be the most venerated Sufi saint of India. There are records of many events of his life. One constant theme is the willing conversion of those who accepted the superiority of his divine power.'[8]

Prof. Harbans Mukhia writes, 'the process of conversions to Islam that took place in India was so slow, spread out over such long stretches of time, and almost imperceptible that the medieval historians, both Hindu and Muslim, failed to notice and record it, except as sporadic events. This implies that conversions did not take place at the hand of one agency or at one go or for one reason, either by use of force or temptation or persuation.'[9] The conversions mostly took place willingly due to the influence and preachings of the sufi saints. Besides, Mukhia shows that more massive conversions took place during the British rule than during the Muslim rule. In the Muslim rule the percentage of Muslims in the heartland of Muslim empire never exceeded 15% of the total population. The slow conversion process explains the persistence of a wide spectrum of pre Islamic some times even anti Islamic, customs ceremonies values and mores among the converts. The Indian Muslims are thus distinctive and a part of that all encompassing civilisation of which tolerance of difference is a central feature.

The Muslim rule ended formally, in India, with the defeat of the last Moghul emperor, Bahadur Shah Zafar by the British in 1857.

After 1857 Muslims faced a lot of persecution at the hands of the British and a great gloom and despondency descended on the community, specially in northern India. M J Akbar writes about this period as follows, 'the clergy lost the battle against the British in nineteenth century. Indian Muslims turned to other avenues, to politics, to education, and as we can see from Iqbal, sometimes even to poetry. Despair has many manifestations. Eventually one of them would become violent.' Different authors have dealt in great detail with the various movements of Indian Muslims in this period. Prior to 1857, the Wahabi movement, which was of religio-political nature was spearheaded by Shah Abdul Aziz and Syed Ahmad Barelvi. It preached puritanical Islam and was anti British. Post 1857, the

Aligarh movement started by Sir Syed was mainly educational. The Deoband movement was religio political. While Sir Syed was pro British, the Deobandis were anti British and influenced by Wahabi heroes. Deoband leaders could not formulate a definite programme of action soon after 1857, though they sided with the Congress. It was Mahmud ul Hasan, the successor of Rasheed Ahmad Gangohi who attempted to provide political and intellectual content to the religious ideal of the Deoband school. He knew that there was need to bring together the Ulema and western educated youth. He wanted to synthesise Islamic principles with national aspirations. Maulana Hussain Ahmad Madani propounded the concept of 'United Nationalism.' 'Ubaidullah Sindhi, trained by Mahmood ul Hasan, was the first Indian Muslim to adopt the nationalist point of view in the interpretation of the history of Islamic world. The most important element of Maulana Sindhi's religious and political thought is humanism. It is drawn from the Quran. According to him this is the real religion; it is close to God; it is above sects, nations, and races. It is the spirit of religion, which is the avenue to the knowledge of God. Mankind is fundamentally one though the sense of unity may be incomplete and hidden. The Quran and other Divine Books are the revelation of this Universal Unity.[10]

In the 20th century Muslims took more actively to politics and the Ali Brothers started the Khilafat Movement. Gandiji lent full support to this movement as a result Hindu Muslim unity increased. Ali brothers joined the Congress. Maulan Azad was also a great nationalist and prominent Congress leader. Under Gandhiji's leadership Muslim men and women took active part in the national struggle for Independence. But the politics of separatism, which was a result of various factors, led to the partition of the nation into secular India and Muslim Pakistan in 1947. A majority of Muslims stayed back in India, their motherland, and were given equal status and rights by the Indian Constitution.

References

1. Singh Yogendra 1973 Modernization of Indian Tradition.
2. Singhal DP. 1971. India and World Civilization Vol. 2. Rupa & Co.
3. MJ Akbar 2002 The Shade of Swords Roli Books.
4. Moin Shakir 1970 Khilafat to Partition Kalamkar Prakashan.
5. Mujeeb 1972 Islamic Influence on Indian Society.
6. Singhal DP. 1971. India and World Civilization Vol. 2 Rupe & Co.
7. Singhal DP. 1971. " " " " " " " " "
8. MJ Akbar 2002. The Shade of Swords Roli Books.
9. Mukhia H Times of India 20.12.2008.
10. Moin Shakir, 1970. Khilafat to Partition Kalamkar Prakashan.

14

Indian Muslims Since Independence

Muslims in India are the biggest minority group, and they form the second largest group of Muslims in a country, in the whole world, after Indonesia. Muslims have a more than a millennium long history in India. The Moghuls were the most powerful Muslim rulers in India and the British snatched power from them in 1857, when the combined Indian troops fighting under the banner of the last Moghul king, Bahadur Shah Zafar, lost against the British forces. In the period between 1857–1947, the Muslims in India went through various turmoils, as they suffered the most after the war. Many movements like the Aligarh Movement, the Deoband Movement, with different ideologies tried to uplift the Muslims in different ways. In the twentieth century, with the starting of the Khilafat Movement Muslim leaders and masses got involved in the national struggle for Independence in great numbers under the leadership of Mahatma Gandhi, because he supported the Khilafat movement and the Ali Brothers joined the Congress and the national struggle for independence. But with Partition, the Indian Muslims once again faced immense suffering and misery. They took a long time to adjust to the existing conditions, and in the absence of a proper and concerned leadership were left rudderless. Nuzhat Sajjad Ali writes, 'Immediately after Independence, the exodus to Pakistan and the carnage that went with it played havoc with the lives of many Muslim families, and it took them a good many years to regain stability. Some did not regain it at all, but succumbed to the devastating conditions. There were others who did not try to emerge out of the abyss of ignorance and poverty, sometimes on account of inertia and indifference and sometimes on account of rigidity and a lop sided view of life. This continues to be the reality of many Muslim families even today. Lack of proper leadership has also been responsible for this backwardness that is more rampant in the North than in the South. The victims of this backwardness are neither aware of true Islam and its teachings,'[1] nor are they aware of modern knowledge, hence there is no improvement. Many books have been written about Indian Muslims which describe in detail the conditions prevailing since pre Independence to present day, I am concentrating on the most contemporary period; i.e. the last three decades.

While India is a remarkably tolerant country and also a vibrant secular democracy, Muslims feel they have faced various amounts of discrimination in different areas and regions on religious grounds. Secondly they also feel they have been branded most unfairly as pro Pakistani and not trusted by some members of the majority community specially in times of crises. This has hurt the feelings of Indian Muslims no end and engendered feelings of frustration, anguish and insecurity among them. The generation who faced the bad times of Partition period lived in a sort of limbo and did not make much progress. The next generation, born in free India was better equipped to face challenges but still remained educationally and economically backward, with some exceptions. For this Muslims themselves are to blame the most although the Government too did not do much to improve their lot except for pandering to the demands of some Muslim leaders. Those Muslims who took advantage of available opportunities prospered but most of them did not make adequate efforts to improve their lot so remained backward. A great number of Muslims lack the will and perseverence to compete and excel, and resort to blaming others for their failure. In the 80s there were some terrible communal riots in cities of Uttar Pradesh like Moradabad and Meerut, which caused lot of misery to Muslims who were affected, besides creating a sense of insecurity and dissatisfaction among Muslims all over the country. The 90s were worse in the sense that Muslims felt more insecure and the tragedy of demolition of Babri Masjid, a national shame, was the last blow. A number of communal riots broke out and some Muslims started resorting to violence in frustration. The Mumbai serial blasts were one such unfortunate occurring. But time being the great healer that it is Muslims did pick up the threads and join the mainstream, in order to survive and prosper. It is not as if no progress was being made in all this time, Muslims were coming up in various fields and making a mark, although in small numbers. An article by B G Verghese entitled Emergence of the Modern Muslim in TOI in 2003 gives a good picture of the condition of Muslims in India in the early 21 st century. He writes, 'A half a century after partition, Muslim Indians are coming into their own. They are no more the psychologically orphaned and beleaguered community they were in the earlier years of Independence. Confident new generations have begun to break out of that mould to find a place in the sun. The decade 1992 – 2002 witnessed the demolition of the Babri Masjid, the war in Afghanistan and the Gujarat Pogrom, bringing renewed trauma and uncertainty. Yet, sullen despair among some was matched by determination among others to assert their civic rights. The message that went out with Talibanization of Afghanistan and international terror culminating in 9/11 caused Islam to be increasingly demonised in the West. Yet in all this time no Muslim Indian was ever found aiding the Taliban or joining the Jehadis or Al Qaida in terrorism in J&K or anywhere else around the world.' He further writes how the genocide in Gujarat, while it was justified by BJP, created feelings of horror and condemnation among millions of non-Muslims, from every part of the country and many reached out in a spirit of caring and compassion; and how the fire was confined to Gujarat and not allowed to spread.

As expected by some, 'Muslims were not forced into ghettos and reduced to supplicants. On the contrary, it has hardened and enlarged the community's resolve to take its due place as Indian citizens demanding their rightful share in the life and fortunes of the country. This has been evident in subtle ways: Quiet conversations, statement, writings, attitudes. The turnaround must be noted, applauded and encouraged.' After this the author has predicted that if the Mumbai blasts are a revenge for Gujarat then this may be a bad development, specially if it is true that educated youth is also involved in terror activities, as is being feared. He also writes that the reason for this may be that when a deeply- wounded community is denied redress, even the sane elements can be moved to desperation.[2] Many other eminent personalities have also commented on the fact that Muslims are unhappy with the discrimination and injustice meted out to them and it is increasing their frustration and may lead to violence. Finance Minister, P Chidambaram, in a lecture in New Delhi has been quoted as saying, 'Out of the hopelessness and despair of the Muslim community - and if not addressed firmly, the Christian tribal communities too – will rise new waves of terror.' [Javed Anand; TOI, 30-9-08] In an article entitled Seven Years After 9/11, B Raman, former Intelligence Officer, writes, 'there are three trends which need to be paid attention to. First, organisations which were already radical due to external [anti-US anger in Pakistan] or internal [anger over domestic grievances in India] reason. Second there is an increase in the flow of new recruits of Muslims to these organisations. Third, we can see the first signs of concern in the Indian Muslim community over this phenomenon. This has led to an open condemnation of terrorism by some leaders of the Muslim community. Anger is the root cause of all terrorism. It is often caused by domestic or external factors. While India may not have much control over external factors, it should be able to detect in time signs of anger due to domestic reasons and take action to address them. Un addressed anger at the domestic level drives the angry into the arms of trans national organisations such as al Quaeda.'[3]

The new generation of Muslims, the youth of the 21st century, are thankfully almost fully integrated into the national mainstream, to the extent that they have no knowledge of Partition and the miseries of that period and consider themselves no different to other Indian youth. An overwhelming majority of them are making use of various opportunities available to them and making progress in different fields. But some misguided youth who are frustrated because of discrimination and general neglect of the community by the authorities, are resorting to violence. As mentioned above there are genuine reasons for the frustration, but redress has to be sought through legitimate means, not by resorting to terror. This new problem of terrorism, that has erupted among some misguided Muslim youth, needs to be condemned strongly and put down immediately. The worst part is that even the educated youth are getting involved in such activities.

Coming to the backwardness of the Muslim community, unfortunately it continues even today. Of course Muslims themselves are to be blamed most for it but the Government also has not given enough support to the community to make progress. The Government has from time to time taken note of this backwardness, by setting up committees to find out its causes, but nothing much has been done to solve the problem by efficiently implementing the suggestions of these committees.

In 1981 a survey was carried out in 139 districts of India, where the Muslim population was found to be between 20% and 95%. The survey presented a dismal picture of backwardness and poverty of the Muslim community in general, and the Muslim women in particular. It showed that the literacy rate of Muslim women was lower than the national female literacy rate. Muslim women form the weakest section of society both educationally and economically.

In 1983 the Gopal Singh Committee declared Muslims as a backward community of India. One factor of this backwardness was their extremely weak social and economic condition. The condition of Muslim women is worse. A majority of them working in the unorganised sector are at the lowest rung of unskilled labour. The percentage in the national labour force is less than 3%. This marginalisation predicts that the percentage must be lower still, for women. This low percentage also shows that Muslims are either not qualified enough or are discriminated against by the employers.[4]

During her tenure as Prime Minister, Smt. Indira Gandhi had presented a 15 Point Programme for Muslims in the 80s after a high level committee set up under Dr Syed Mahmood had presented its report.

In 1995 the NDA Government had also ordered the National Minority Commission to present a Report about Muslims based on a survey.

After the demolition of the Babri Masjid there were serious repercussions and communal riots resulted in many places. But after a period of rehabilitation and reconciliation, Muslims started joining the mainstream once again in increasing numbers, specially the educated youth and started prospering.

In the 21st century, President A P J Abdul Kalam announced to the Parliament in his address on 25th February 2005 that the Government will prepare a new and better 15 Point Programme for the welfare of minorities. On 15th August 2005 Prime Minister Manmohan Singh announced the introduction of the New 15 Point Programme. According to the Programme wherever there is a substantial population of Muslims and other minority groups, in the entire country, then it is the duty of the administration and the State Government to provide a minimum of 15% of the benefits of the following Government of India Welfare

Schemes to the minorities the Schemes included in this list are ICDS Projects, including pre school, health and nutrition facilities, Sarva Shiksha Abhiyan, appointment of Urdu teachers where more than 25% population is urdu peaking, Modernization of Madrasas, Employment schemes like SGRY, SGSY, and NREGS and also special consideration by State Governments to recruit minorities in Police Force, 15% allocation for Muslims living below Poverty Line in rural areas for Indira Awas Yojna, and in slum development schemes in urban areas. Besides measures to reduce communal tension, appointment of neutral officers in sensitive areas, provision of relief to riot victims and proper rehabilitation were also mentioned in the Programme.

On 9th March the PMO notified that a High Level Committee was being constituted to prepare a report on the social, economic and educational status of the Muslim community of India because a lack of authentic information on the above aspects comes in the way of planning, formulating and implementing specific interventions, policies and programmes, to address the issues relating to backwardness of Muslims. Justice Rajender Sachar was appointed the Chairperson and Dr Abu Saleh Shariff, the Member Secretary, besides five other members.

The Sachar Committee Report was presented on 30th November, 2006 in the Parliament.

The main findings of the Committee were, 'the Muslim community exhibits deficits and deprivation in practically all dimensions of development. In fact, by and large, Muslims rank somewhat above SCs /STs but below Hindu OBCs, other minorities and Hindu General [mostly upper castes] categories in almost all indicators considered. Among the states that have large Muslim populations, the situation is particularly grave for e.g. in the states of West Bengal, Bihar, UP and Assam.'

The main recommendations of the Sachar Committee Report were:

1. Designate Arzal Muslim groups as Most backward class, as they need multifarious measures including reservation.
2. Provide Ajlaf Muslim groups Hindu OBC type attention.
3. Provide financial and other support to initiatives built around occupations where Muslims are concentrated and that have growth potential.
4. Increase employment share of Muslims particularly where there is great deal of public dealing.
5. Set up an Equal Opportunity Commission to look into grievances of deprived groups like minorities
6. Provide legal mechanism to address complaints of discriminations against minorities in matters of employment, housing, schooling, obtaining bank loans.
7. Work out nomination procedure to increase participation of minorities in public bodies.
8. Recognise degrees from Madrasas for eligibility in defence, civil and banking institutions
9. Work out mechanisms to link madrasas with higher secondary school boards.
10. Promote and enhance access to Muslims in priority sector advances
11. Draw Muslims on relevant interview panels and boards. Improve participation and share of minorities, particularly Muslims in business of regular commercial banks.
12. Set up a national Wakf Development Corporation with a revolving corpus of Rs. 5 billion.[5]

Evaluating the progress made in implementing the Sachar Committee recommendations, Mujibur Rahman, who teaches at Jamia Millia Islamia, writes, 'The UPA government has selectively endorsed the Sachar recommendations, while some are still under consideration. For instance setting up of an equal opportunity commission and a national data bank are yet to be taken up.' He further writes that although every year more money has been allotted for minority development, there is a lack of proper monitoring and evaluation of implementation of various programmes. Secondly separate initiatives should be taken for education of Muslim girls. Muslims should be encouraged to set up civil society groups as recommended by Sachar Committee.[6] The author feels that Muslims themselves have to take an initiative and seek government's help and guidance if it is not forthcoming. Dr Syed Hamid, a renowned educationist and member of Sachar Committee also says that Muslims themselves should work for their betterment and use all the facilities available and demand all those privileges and rights which are not available to improve their lot.

In the last few years the serious problem of terrorism has unfortunately cast a dark cloud over the prospects of Indian Muslims, who were already burdened with the problems arising out of communal tensions and riots in the wake of demolition of Babri Masjid and resultant Hindu revivalism. More recently Muslims of Indian origin are being accused for terrorist activities. While some accusations are true, some are baseless and Muslim youth are harassed by the police on vague suspicions and then let off after ruining their reputation and careers. It is true that even if a few misguided Muslims are resorting to terrorist activities, it is very wrong and condemnable. Muslim leaders and Ulema are condemning it very vehemently. The worst thing is that the terrorists are trying to justify their misdeeds by calling it Jehad. The meaning of Jehad has been thoroughly discussed in the previous chapter. Terrorist activities are definitely not Jehad. The media is also responsible for using the word Jehadis for the terrorists; this creates a general impression that only Muslims are terrorists. There have terrorists of various religions in India. The Sikh extremists were first termed terrorists. Amulya Ganguly writes, 'Incidentally, the Hindutva group never mentions that the ULFA and LTTE terrorists are Hindus and that the latter were inventors of suicide bombing before the jehadis,'[7] although he has also named the terrorists, as jehadis. MJ Akbar rightly writes, 'Terrorists have inflicted the greatest damage on those in whose name they pretend to act, Indian Muslims. Already burdened by multiple anxieties, Indian Muslim youth are now frozen in the headlights of suspicion, and thus easy fodder for a police force that exploits suspicion to harass a community instead of eliminating criminals.'[8] 'The front page of Nai Duniya Weekly, an Urdu weekly, ran the headline: 'Back to back blasts; a conspiracy to pit the nation against Muslims; these devils [terrorists] cant be Muslims', on September 15th 2008, two days after the Delhi bomb blasts.'[9] Recently the National Minority Commission has also refuted the charge of the MP Government that the SIMI was behind the July riots. The news item says; 'Rubbishing MP government's contention that SIMI was behind the July riots in Indore, the National Commission for Minorities has dubbed the claim as 'mischievous' Noting that the root cause of the violence lies in the Bandh call by VHP, the panel said MP government could have taken suo motu action against the bandh as the SC has already declared Bandhs as unconstitutional.'[10] The recent encounter in Jamia Nagar in Delhi, killing two Muslim youth, in connection with the blasts, is also under the scanner to prove it wasn't a fake encounter, as there have been many, earlier, in Gujarat and Maharashtra involving Muslim suspects. While criminals of majority community are let off easily, the criminals of minority communities are tortured and punished, sometimes even with out reason. Sujata Patel, a

Professor in Pune University has created an on line archive on human rights violations in India, and she says in an interview, 'The 50 odd documents on democracy and law, in the archive, discuss in detail POTA and TADA and highlight how these 'tough laws'were misused. They show how the Police, with the support of those in power, picked up innocent citizens under these laws, often tortured and sometimes eliminated them through 'encounters'. Most of those targeted were from the minorities, or were Dalits or Adivasi.'[11] On October 22nd 2008, the ATS of the Maharashtra Police declared that it has convincing proof of members of fundamentalist Hindutva groups like ABVP being responsible for Malegaon and Modasa blasts in September 2008, and not members of SIMI as had been told earlier. In a report in Times of India it is said that the Anti Terror Squad of Mumbai Police have so far detained five persons linked to Indore city in connection with Malegaon and Modasa blasts. Mumbai police has claimed that all five persons are connected to saffron organizations – the Hindu Jagran Manch, BJP, RSS and ABVP. Three people have also been arrested in this regard.[12] All such news as well as the frequency and ease with which such acts are occurring, and the swiftness with which police is solving the cases and arresting alleged criminals, lends some credence to the theory that is forwarded by the Urdu Press and some sections of the Muslim community that it may be a conspiracy against Muslims. It is also possible that some Muslims are being used by vested interests to resort to terror activities for monetary consideration, while many innocent Muslim youth are being unnecessarily arrested on flimsy grounds. Be that as it may, Muslims in India are passing through a tough period and will have to face the challenge and prove their worth as Indians. India is as much their homeland as it is of any one else and they should be proud of it and bring a good name to it. They should have faith in the country's legal system. No matter how much wrong has been done to you, if you are a true Muslim you should have faith in God and not resort to underhand means to seek redress. Truth will prevail in the end, if one has patience to continue on the right path. Secondly as a citizen of India, you owe allegiance to your country and are honour bound to be loyal. A Muslim always keeps his word and promise.

An article in Times of India entitled, Is There A Muslim Mindset? discusses how life has become insecure and difficult for the community in the wake of frequent terrorist activities. The author, Mohammad Wajihuddin, quotes an urdu journalist, Hasan Kamal as follows, 'Just after Independence Muslims were afraid to keep Urdu books in their homes lest they were labelled as Pakistani sympathisers. After the 1971 war the community shook off the guilt it had been carrying since the days of Partition. Now Muslims are once again being made to feel guilty- this time they are seen as sympathetic to the bombers.' The author further writes that the Muslim community has had many grievances. It has not benefited from India's rapid economic progress, which makes matters worse; but the cause of Muslim anger is not deprivation alone. It is also the sense of Justice discriminating against them. While Muslims are arrested without any restraint after a riot, non Muslims are generally let off, be it in the Mumbai riots of 1993 or the Gujarat riots of 2002. When the state discriminates against a section of its citizens, it prepares fertile ground for retaliation.'

'It is obvious the agencies go soft when it comes to blast cases involving Hindu organizations. 'In Nanded in April 2006 two Bajrang Dal workers were killed while making crude bombs. A similar incident took place in Kanpur in 2008, but the authorities did not take any action,' says Ram Punyani, an activist.'[13]

The only redeeming feature for Muslims, in the article above seems to be that non-Muslims like Ram Punyani are ready to fight for their cause. There are many other such activists in India who speak for justice and human rights regardless of their religious affiliation and this is definitely due to the age- old tradition of tolerance in India. Here it is also worth noting that Indian Muslims too have shown their solidarity with the nation by condemning the terrorists to a person. Even the parents of suspected terrorists have said publicly that they were not aware of the activities of their children, but if they are found to be guilty they should be punished according to the law. In fact, in the words of Zafar ul Islam Khan, Muslims in India want a common criminal law for all so that all citizens are treated similarly for the same offence.

Another problem faced by Muslims in most cities is that they are discriminated against when it comes to buying or renting houses in Hindu areas. This leads to ghettoisation for which they are blamed. They are forced to live in totally Muslim localities, not because they want to. The biggest ghetto of Juhapura in Gujarat is one example. Secondly civic facilities are not provided properly in these areas and Muslims are blamed for being dirty and unhygienic. Banks do not open branches in these localities nor do offer loans to the residents. J.S. Bandookwala writes Muslims must improve these areas on then own. He laments that Muslim dignitaries hardly do anything to encourage Muslim Masses. (EPW April 8-14, 2006).

The centres of traditional Muslim education, the Madrasas are also under the scanner and are being dubbed as breeding grounds for terrorists; a charge which is strongly refuted by the clerics and teachers at the Madrasas. The most famous Madrasa the Dar ul Uloom Deoband has a history of nationalism and patriotism. Recently it has condemned all terrorist activities in the name of religion, as very wrong and un Islamic. Here we present excerpts from the interview of Maulana Margoob ur Rehman, the rector of Asia's oldest seminary, the Dar ul Uloom Deoband which was conducted by Firoz Bakht Ahmad in March 2003 He said there is nothing to defend against the charges of VHP and their likes because 'we are like an open book. I cordially invite anyone to visit without prior notice and attend all our classes and take rounds and inspect and assess if any terrorists are being sheltered here or if anyone is manufacturing weapons. We don't train people even for self defence. In the 137 years of our existence, we have produced 76,000 graduates. We ought to get kudos for producing simple, educated, law abiding people. Instead our values are being questioned. The allegation that Madrasas preach obscurantism smacks of ignorance. All madrasa students live as per the dictates of their religion, which teaches them to be happy in the little they have and not be covetous.' He goes on to say that probably people do not know that the Dar ul Uloom was among the first to give the call for liberation of India from British rule. Its 'Reshmi Rumaal Tehreek' which included leaders like Maulana Mehmood ul Hasan, Maulana Abul Kalam Azad and Khan Abdul Ghaffar Khan was a movement against the British. Finally he said, 'I have openly castigated the heinous acts of Jaish e Mohammad, Lashkar-e-Toiba and other such terrorist platforms that have endangered the existence of Muslims in India because of their lop sided interpretation of jehad and killing of innocent people. I am ashamed of those who use Islam to carry out acts of terror.'[14] In spite of such open condemnation Muslims are still considered as pro terrorists and looked upon with suspicion. This is a big problem for ordinary citizens who are just like any other Indian wanting to live in peace.

In order to solve all these problems Muslims will have to work very hard and also win the support of the majority community for this purpose. As long as there is an atmosphere of mistrust, things will not improve much. Muslims have to educate themselves, increase their general awareness, try to mingle with open heart with other countrymen and give up some of their old habits and beliefs which are not based on Islamic teachings instead are unauthenticated traditions passed from one generation to the other as a matter of course. Hindus will have to lend a helping hand to their fellow country men and trust them, because after all they are also Indians and if they remain backward, the whole country will suffer Hindus have always been very broad minded and tolerant, and many continue to do so even today. They have to realise that co existence is a must and the more peaceful it is the better.

Some constructive efforts both by Muslims and non Muslims to improve the lot of the minorities are being made. Muslim women are also trying to improve their lot in many ways. There are many NGOs working exclusively to promote the awareness of Muslim women and help them improve their lot. One such organisation in Uttarakhand is Disha which is doing commendable work for the last twenty five year among rural Muslim women. Muslim women themselves are making efforts to break old shackles, placed on them by custom, contrary to teachings of Islam, and exercise their rights. One such example is the setting up of All India Muslim Women Personal Law Board which was set up after breaking away from the parent body, the AIMPLB because women felt it was gender biased. Shaista Amber, President of this new Board has drafted a woman friendly Nikahnama, called the Sharai Nikahnama, with the help of a 30 member executive body and presented it on 16th March 2008. The Nikahnama makes registration of the marriage compulsory and also bans Triple Talaq and insists on prompt payment of Mehr. But the clerics are not accepting this document as binding. Ambar is hopeful that gradually people will accept it.[15]

There are secular organisations that are working for the welfare of the down- trodden including Muslims and other minorities. e.g. SEWA There are also anti communal organisations that came up in the 80s to counter the Hindutva perceptions that secularism appeases Muslims and the Muslim community is pampered. Eg. Sampradayikta Virodhi Andolan in 1985 Then there are organisations headed by Muslims that represent the Muslim perspective like AIMPLB set up in 1972 or the All India Milli Council set up in 1992. Besides these three types of organisations there are many Muslim organisations which work for the educational and social uplift of Muslims in their region, like the Education Societies in south Indian states or the AIBMM set up by Eijaz Ali in 1994 in Bihar and Jan Chatna an NGO set up in Ahmadabad.[16] Besides all these there are organisations set up by the Government, like the National Minority Commission, the Waqf Board and the National Human Rights Commission which are all working for welfare of minorities and down trodden sections of society. The National Minority Commission was set up to evaluate the progress of the development of the minorities, to monitor the working of safeguards provided in the Constitution, to make recommendations for effective implementation of safeguards for protection of interests of minorities, to look into complaints of minorities and to conduct studies to find out problems of minorities and suggest solutions. It has the powers of a Civil court trying a suit, summoning any Indian and examining him on oath. It can ask for relevant documents to be produced and issue commissions for examination of witness and documents.

It is not easy to comment in a comprehensive way about the status or condition of Muslims in contemporary India because they are not one monolith but a highly differentiated heterogeneous population, with different attitudes, thoughts and even ideologies. Some are prospering, while a majority are suffering due to negligence, marginalization and also their own fault. Everyone will have to make individual efforts to improve and not wait for others to do something for them. One must learn to shoulder ones responsibilities and then demand ones rights, as a citizen of India, whatever one's religion be. India is a secular country and will have to provide for all, albeit after a lot of procrastination. For nothing is it said, 'where there is a will there is a way', or 'if you want you can!' Indian Muslims should believe in such maxims and try their best to get their due by correct and peaceful means. No doubt it is not an easy job but nothing is impossible if one really works hard for it. Muslims specially, believe that when man makes an effort Allah definitely helps him, 'Himmat-e-mardan madad-e- Khuda', so it should be that much more easier for them to be motivated for hard work. Its high time Muslims in India adopted positive thinking and positive actions instead of negative ones to over come their short comings.

REFERENCES

1. Sajjad Ali Nuzhat 1998 Muslim Women Since Independence Institute of Objective Studies.
2. Varghese BG TOI September 22nd 2003.
3. Raman B TOI 'Seven year after 9/11' 11th September 2008.
4. Souvenir of Insaf Conference (2007) Gaya Bihar.
5. Ibid.
6. Mujibur Rahman TOI March 19th 2008.
8. M J Akbar TOI September 21st 2008.
9. News Item TOI September 21st 2008.
10. News Item TOI October 7th 2008.
11. Patel Sujata TOI October 13th 2008.
12. News Item TOI October 25th 2008.
13. Wajihuddin TOI September 21st 2008.
14. Firoz Bakht Ahmad 'Defender of Faith', TOI March 24th 2003.
15. Mishra Manjri TOI March 19th 2008.
16. EPW Yamini Aiyar & Meeto Malik Oct 23rd –29th 2004.

15

Conclusion

An attempt was made in the preceding chapters to establish that all religions are basically the same except for variations in some details which are time specific and area specific, because the Supreme Being Who created the Universe and the human beings is One and the same and has sent His messengers from time to time with His Eternal Message of right and wrong. The Quran is the final Word of the Supreme Being sent to the entire humanity through an Arabic Prophet, since no prophet had been sent in that area for a long time. The Quran confirms all previous religious traditions and enjoins men to believe in all messengers of the Supreme Being, Who is called by different names by different people. In Arabic He is called Allah, just as He is called God in English and Om in Sanskrit. The Eternal religion of the Almighty is One. In Arabic it is known as Islam which means surrender to the Will of the Almighty. Islam teaches people to do good in order that they are rewarded for it in the Hereafter. The word 'Deen' has also been used for the eternal religion in Quran, as the following quotation shows: Surah 30 verse 30 'So set thou thy face truly to the religion [Deen] being upright [Haneef], the nature in which Allah has made mankind; No change [there is] in the work [wrought] by Allah. That is the true religion [Deen]: but most among mankind know not.' The Quran argues that this Deen is the only true religion in the following verse. Allah says, 'Do they seek for other than the Religion of Allah – while all creatures in the heaven and the earth have, willing or unwilling, bowed to His Will [accepted Islam], and to Him shall they all be brought back.' The Quran specifies all that constitutes 'good' and should be followed and also explains what is evil and should be avoided. Allah Himself proclaims that the Quran is His Word and He Himself will protect it always. That the Quran is a revelation from the Almighty is proclaimed many times in the Quran, for instance 'As for thee [Mohammad] thou receivest the Quran from One All Wise, All Knowing.' [Surah 27 verse 6] The Quran is praised as follows by Allah : 'The Word of the Lord doth find its fulfilment in truth and in justice: none can change His words: for He is the One Who heareth and knoweth all.' [Surh 6 verse 115]

The Quran also gives detailed accounts of various aspects of life, creation of the universe, history of humanity, description of the Hereafter and the Day of Judgement and many other issues. In short it is a comprehensive guide for human beings and its teachings are relevant for all time to come, if we interpret them in their broadest or basic sense. In the second chapter we have seen how researchers have found similarities and also some differences in the various religious traditions of the world and concluded finally that all religions convey the same message with some variations. Here the author would like to comment on some other similarities that have been observed by her or related to her by others. The story of Prophet Noah as given in Bible and the Quran is similar to the story of Manu and the great destruction or Pralay as recounted in the Hindu tradition. Similarly the story of Prahlad's childhood when there was an attempt to burn him is similar to the story of Prophet Abraham's childhood when the evil king tried to burn him. In either case the fire did not harm the innocent boy, because the Almighty wanted to save him. These instances show that probably these are the same events of history that are being repeated variously by various peoples. Some verses of the Vedas and the Quran are very similar as shown in the second chapter. Of course there are too many similarities in the contents of the Quran and the Bible and Gospel, because they share a common history. In India we see that the Sikh religion is an amalgamation of the Muslim and the Hindu traditions and draws extensively from both. The poetry of Amir Khusro, Kabir and others also presents a synthesis of various religious traditions. One Doha of Sant Kabir appears to be the exact replica of Quranic verses. Kabir says, 'Sab dharti kagad karoon, lekhani sab ban rai, saat samund ki masi karoon, harigun likha na jai.' The Quran says, 'And if all the trees on earth were pens and the oceans [were ink] with seven oceans behind it to add to its [supply], yet would not the Words of Allah be exhausted [in the writing]: for Allah is exalted in Power, full of Wisdom.' [Surah 31 verse 27]

The Sufi Tradition in Islam has also been a very important source of uniting different religious traditions. Asghar Ali Engineer, writes, 'Believing in the unity of all beings, most Sufis did not harbour a hostile or sectarian attitude towards other faiths. This liberal doctrine leads the Sufis to assert that the Real Being is Allah and that the entire universe, including human beings, are His creation and hence any distinction between the two would be artificial. The founder of this doctrine, Mohiuddin ibn Arabi, used to say, 'My heart is a mosque, a temple, a church and a synagogue. God is love and my heart is the seat of love.' The Sufis were the messengers of love and advocated the principle of Sulh-e-kul-peace with all and conflict with none. Thus Sufism is a bridge of understanding between faiths.'[1] Some Sufi Thoughts as recorded by sufiorder. org also show how they preach unity of religion, for instance: 'There is One God, the Eternal, the Only Being; none exists save He'; 'There is One Holy Book, the sacred manuscript of nature, the only scripture that can enlighten the reader,' and 'There is One Religion, the unswerving progress in the right direction towards the ideal, which fulfils the life's purpose of every soul' and finally, 'There is One Path, the annihilation of the false ego in the real, which raises the mortal to immortality, in which resides all perfection.'[2] The One Holy Book mentioned in the Quran as the Mother of All Books, is with God, safe in the Loh e Mahfooz, and it is said again and again in the Quran that there is only One Path which leads to the right goal.

The next chapter discusses the relevance of Quranic teachings in modern times for the entire humanity. In this chapter, besides presenting guidelines for good behaviour in daily life and admonition for various evil practices, the author has concentrated on Quranic pronouncements on contemporary issues like female infanticide, prostitution, alcoholism, cheating in business and hoarding. Quranic verses that provide solace to man and thus reduce his stress and depression are also quoted extensively. All this goes to show that Quran has great relevance for the modern man and it is up to him to read it, follow it and derive inspiration and solace from it. Allah has proclaimed often in the Quran that man should ponder on the Quranic verses and learn from them. In Surah Qamar, one verse has been repeated again and again which says, 'And We have indeed made the Quran easy to understand and remember: then is there any that will receive admonition?' [Surah 54 verse 17].

The next chapter describes the characteristics of true believers, be they known by any religious denomination. Once again, the author has described what is considered right behaviour and what is considered bad behaviour according to the Quran, but in this chapter not only secular matters but religious obligations of true believers are also included. A true believer is one who believes in One Supreme Being, His Books, His Prophets, His Angels and in the Day of Judgement. The Quran says, 'Nay – whoever submits his whole self to Allah and is a doer of good, - he will get his reward with his Lord; on such shall be no fear, nor shall they grieve.' [Surah 2 verse 112] or again, "Those who believe [in the Quran], those who follow the Jewish [scriptures] and the Sabians and the Christians – any who believe in Allah and the Last Day, and work righteousness-on them shall be no fear, nor shall they grieve." [Surah 5 verse 69]

There are separate chapters on the position of women in Islam, marriage and family in Islam, the concept of Jehad in Islam and Quranic pronouncements about Jews and Christians. These are some of the most discussed and contemporary issues hence they were dealt in detail. The position of women in Islam is very respectable and important although it is not the same as that of man. This is because Quran says they complement each other and hence have their own strengths and weaknesses. Women have all the rights that men have, albeit with some variations. Both men and women are equally responsible for their actions and will be rewarded or punished in the same way on the Day of Judgement. Details of marriage and family also show that both men and women are equally important and have their rights and obligations; but men have an upper hand because they are the providers and the protectors. These teachings are similar to the teachings of other religious books, because after all they are all from the same Supreme Being. Depending on the time and space there are some variations and Quran being the Last Message from the Supreme Being, it removes many earlier hindrances and grants more rights and privileges, to the oppressed[in this case women]

Unfortunately Jehad has become a very sinister word in modern times and some misguided Muslims have brought a bad name to it and also to Islam by equating it with violence and terrorism. Learned Muslims, both religious leaders and secular persons, have denounced terrorist activities of so called Muslims and clarified that terrorism is not Jehad. Jehad is striving for betterment, both mentally and physically. If some one is being oppressed or is in danger of being killed for his religious principles, he can resort to fighting; but he cannot kill innocent people nor can he create tumult. There are well defined rules for fighting oppression. Fighting for the cause of the oppressed is also Jehad, which Gandhiji undertook in South Africa, being inspired by a Quranic verse. The more common and important form of Jehad is to try and improve oneself spiritually.

One of the main grouses of the Jews and Christians is that they are mentioned in the Quran in a derogatory way. This is far from the truth. The Quran hails the Jews as the Chosen people of God, but it admonishes those Jews who strayed from the right path and forgot the teachings of their Prophets. There are Surahs dedicated to the Jews and their Prophets in the Quran and Allah tells about all the favours He bestowed on the Jews. The importance of good Jews even in the time of Prophet Mohammad is obvious from the following quotation: 'Without doubt it [Quran] is [announced] in the revealed Books of former peoples. Is it not a Sign to them [Arabs] that the Learned of the Children of Israel knew it [as true]? [Surah 26 verses 196 –197] About the Christians the Quran says they are very learned, caring and not arrogant [Surah 5 verse 82] Those Christians who believe in the Quran and testify that it is the Word of God and also believe in Prophet Mohammad are praised in the Quran. The Quran says such people will be rewarded doubly. [Surah 28 verses 52 –54] and [Surah 17 verses 107- 108] There is a Surah dedicated to Mary the mother of Jesus and a Surah dedicated to Jesus and his miracles, [Surah Maida] in the Quran. The Quran admonishes those Christians who started calling Prophet Jesus as the Son of God, because it is not true. Jesus never claimed to be the Son of God. This was added to the Christian faith after the death of Jesus, when Rome adopted it as the official religion.

There is a chapter on some of the common themes of the Quran which are repeated again and again, in order to stress their importance and make them clear to human intelligence. It is very difficult for anyone to write comprehensively about the Holy Quran, because it is full of so much knowledge and truth that it is not possible for an ordinary individual to encompass it entirely. Secondly everyone is able to understand only according to his/her intellect and with special guidance from Allah. The author is no authority on religion but has always strived to understand the Holy Book to the best of her ability. Her late father who is the co author also did the same all his life. Both were inspired to do so by the Quranic verse, 'And We have indeed made the Quran easy to understand and remember: then is there any that will receive admonition?' [Surah 54 verse 40]. An attempt has been made to cover as many relevant topics as possible in this book which tries to spread the teachings of Quran among humanity. Therefore in the chapter on oft repeated themes, only some important topics are dealt with. These were selected either because of their contemporary significance or to show the practical and human side of Quranic teachings. The Quran gives details about the creation of the universe and the purpose behind it. It also gives details of how human beings disobey and disbelieve the teachings of God and prove ungrateful. It also describes how people differ from each other and how they will be judged according to their different actions and beliefs. It is said again and again in the Quran that if He so wished Allah would have made all people alike and there would be no distinctions; but He made them different so that they may be judged accordingly.

There is one chapter on the condition of Indian Muslims, specially in the last three decades. This again is so vast a subject that one cannot do justice to it even in one book leave alone one chapter. The author has tried to focus on the common national issues related to social and economic life of Muslims and not gone into regional or other specific issues. Many books have been written about Indian Muslims, giving details of their history and the events leading to Partition and their position in Independent India. For instance, S Abid Husain, former VC of Jamia Millia has written a good book entitled The Destiny of Indian Muslims. In this book he gives a detailed account of the condition of Indian Muslims in the early decades of independence and the challenges facing them. He writes, 'there is a fetishist school of nationalism and patriotism which prescribes some sort of religious devotion to the nation and the country and worship them like deities. No Muslim would subscribe to any such faith.' He goes on to write that while Muslims cannot equate the nation to God, it is their duty to love their motherland like their own mother, be loyal to their country and State and be prepared to sacrifice anything, except their religion and culture, for the security, honour and dignity of their country. 'Indian Muslims should have true faith in One God and His Divine Attributes, should realize in themselves the moral values of Islam and should be able to take an effective part in raising the moral level of their own people and country as well as of the whole of mankind.' He laments that instead of this, Indian Muslims have feeble faith and their actions are devoid of the true spirit of religion and morality. He opines that a religious re awakening is required to inspire the Muslims.[3] Such a reawakening did take place in the 70s when the contact with Middle East and Saudi Arabia increased, but before it could bear positive results, there was a simultaneous reawakening among Hindus which unfortunately led finally, to the demolition of the Babri Masjid. Since then polarisation of the two communities has continued and extremists on both sides have done a lot of harm to the nation and its unity.

In the last two decades, after the demolition of the Babri Mosque, Indian Muslims have felt really hurt and faced too many problems. Some of them have reacted in a wrong way and hence deserve punishment but the vast majority who remained loyal and peaceful has also been punished in the sense that it has been discriminated against and treated unjustly on some occasions. To add insult to injury the Hindutva groups shout themselves hoarse by saying the minorities have always been appeased. If they had been appeased they would have been in a much better socio economic condition than they are in now, as shown by the Report of Sachar Committee. Some minority leaders may have been appeased, from time to time, by political parties of different hues, in order to win their support, but in no way has that benefited the community. The Muslim community itself is also to be blamed for its backwardness. They have to make a concerted effort to utilise all the facilities that are provided by the State to all citizens and improve their condition. They should demand better facilities for themselves in an organised and legal way from the authorities. They should rise above petty issues and vote for development in all elections. At present Muslims vote in a very emotional way and hence do not benefit in any concrete way after the results. In this respect M J Akbar has very rightly written that, 'Fettered by fear, Muslims fritter away their vote.' He has analysed the Muslim thinking which is narrow and dominated by fear factor. Instead, he writes, Muslims should be positive and demand equality in all development processes. The example of Kerala Muslims, who consider themselves as equal to other citizens and hence are treated as such, should be an eye opener for other Muslim groups.[4] Muslims should concentrate on educating themselves, improving their skills and interacting with their fellowmen to learn new things and benefit through them. Interacting with others and becoming familiar with each other improves social relations among different groups. There is tremendous scope for Muslims to make progress in our country, provided they set their hearts to achieve success through hard work. Muslims have made the right decision by denouncing perpetrators of all forms of violence and terror, from all platforms. They have shown great sagacity and maturity by doing so, specially in the face of irrational and highly biased responses by Hindutva brigade regarding terror attacks carried out by Hindus. Instead of condemning they have defended the perpetrators and senior BJP leaders have said it is not in the genes of Hindus to resort to terror! This, after the instances of burning alive of the missionary Staines and his children and killing of innocent Muslims in Gujarat and Christians in Orrisa by Hindus, seems ridiculous.

On the other hand, Muslim clergy and laymen have categorically denounced all terrorists. On 8th Nov 2008, 6000 Ulema denounced terrorism at the 29th Conference of the Jamiat-e-Ulama e Hind at Hyderabad. After the dastardly attacks in Mumbai in November 2008, all Muslim religious organisations spoke vehemently against terrorism and condemned Pakistan's attempts to involve the name of Darul Uloom Deoband in influencing the activities of Pakistani militants. Similarly they refuted Pakistan's claim that the Mumbai attacks were to avenge the wrong done to Indian Muslims. Muslim leader, Zafar-ul-Islam Khan said Indian Muslims are quite satisfied with their condition and can fight for their own rights with out any outsiders' help. This is the correct spirit. Indian Muslims have a future only as Indians and it is in India that they will prosper by their efforts and the help of their countrymen.

The author would like to point out that following the basic tenets of one's religion and observing religious practices with proper faith is always beneficial to man, whatever faith he may follow. Religion gives a new strength to a man; he feels the Almighty is helping him. In modern times being religious should not prevent a person from fighting for his rights and standing up against injustice. Being meek and patient is correct only to a certain extent but it should not make a person passive. Religion should, in fact, encourage a person to act in the right direction and achieve success both in worldly and otherworldly pursuits. Recent studies and trends also show that belief in Almighty reduces stress and antisocial behaviour. Religion should not be confined to rituals but should apply to every day life.

Finally the author would once again like to quote from the Quran to show that all religions are the same and there is unity of mankind. The Supreme Being has created the Universe with some purpose and He knows how the Universe will end. He has shown the right path to the people again and again and it is up to the people to follow it. God helps those to follow the right path who seek His guidance. The following quotation explains this fully. "The same religion has He established for you as that which He enjoined on Noah – that which We have sent by inspiration to thee— and that which We enjoined on Abraham, Moses and Jesus : namely that ye should remain steadfast in religion [Deen], and make no divisions therein. To those who worship, other things than Allah, hard is the [way] to which thou callest them. Allah chooses to Himself those whom He pleases, and guides to Himself those who turn [to Him].' [42:13]

TRANSLATION

Abdullà Yusuf Ali.

References

1. Engineer Asghar Ali, 'Sufism' TOI Oct. 2003.
2. Sufi thoughts, Times of India, 23 Oct. 2008.
3. Hussain Abid S. 1965 The Destiny of Indian Muslims Asia Publishing House.
4. MJ Akbar, Times of India. 'The Siege Within' 14 Dec., 2008.

Bibliography

TRANSLATIONS

1. Marmaduke Pickthall Holy Quran English Translation
2. Dawood NJ 1978 The Quran A Translation Allen Lane London
3. Abdullah Yusuf Ali 2007 Holy Quran English Translation Adam Publishers
4. Mohd. Taqiuddin Hilali & Mohd. Mohin Khan 2002 The Noble Quran English Translation Darussalam Publihers. Arabia

BOOKS

1. Amir Ali Syed 1955 The Spirit of Islam London.
2. Troll W Christian 1982 Ilam in India Vikas Publishing House.
3. Hitti Philip K 1970 Islam a way of life OUP.
4. Mujeeb M 1967 The Indian Mulims London.
5. Mujeeb M 1972 Islamic Influence on Indian Society.
6. Menon Indu 1981 Status of Muslim Women in India Uppal Publishing.
7. Husain Abid S. 1965 Destiny of Indian Muslims Asia Publishing House.
8. Khan Zafarullah M. 1980. ISLAM-Its meaning for Modern Man. Routledge & Kegan Paul.
9. Singh Yogendra Modernization of Indian Tradition (1973) Manohar.
10. Rahman Zainab 2005 Women and Society Kalpaz Publications.
11. Imran 1998 Calling to Islam IREF Hyderabad.
12. Hashia Haseena 1998. Muslim Women in India since Independence. Institute of Object.

13. Pachauri & Chakkanatt (Ed) 2004 Religion Cultural Purality & Nation State. ive Studies.
14. Bhatt GS 2003 Sociology of Religion Unit 19 Hinduism IGNOU Publication.
15. Woodsmall Ruth Frances 1983 Women in the Changing Islamic System Bimla Publication.
16. Smith Wilfred Cantwell 1957 Islam in Modern History Publication University Press.
17. Akbar MJ 2002. The Shade of Swords Role Books.
18. Zakaria Rafiq 2000. Discovery of God. Popular Prakashan.
19. Maulana Abul Kalam Azad 2006 Edition Tarjumanul Quran. Maulana Azad Research Institute Delhi.
20. Kapadia Marriage and Family in India (1966) Oxford University Press.
21. The Last Two Million Years 1973 Reader's Digest Association.
22. Rahman Zainab 1995 Unpublished Ph.D. Thesis Muslims in the Changing Scenario—A Case Study in Dehradun.
23. Ahmad Imtiaz (Ed) 1983, Modernization and Social Change Among Muslims Manohar Prakashan.
24. Attar Farid al Din 1996. Muslim Saints and Mystics, translated by Arberry Routledge and Kegan Paul London.
25. Baveja Malik Ram 1988. Women in Islam Renaissance Pubglishing House Delhi.
26. Bhatia B.M. 1970. History and Social Development Vol. I Vikas Publishers.
27. Engineer A.A. 1985. Islam and Muslims—A Critical Assessment Printwell Publishers.
28. Fayzee A.A.A. 1963. A Modern Approach to Islam.
29. Nanda B.R. (Ed.) 1968. Indian Women—From Purdah to Modernity Vikas Publishers.
30. Qutb Mohammad 1964. Islam the Misunderstood Religion. The Board of Islamic Publications Jama Masjid Delhi.

31. Siddiqui M.M. 1980. Women in Islam Adam Publishers.
32. Singhal D.P. 1971. India and World Civilization Vol. 2, Rupa & Co.
33. Shareef Jafar 1951. Islam in India, Oxford University Press.
34. Shushtery A.M.A. 1938. Outlines of Islamic Culture Vol. 2, Bangalore Press.
35. Shakir Moin 1970. Khilafat to Partition, Kalamkar Prakashan.
36. Shakir Moin 1972. Muslims in Free India, Kalamkar Prakashan.
37. Tarachand 1936. Influence of Islam on Indian Culture. The India Press, Allahabad.

Newspapers and Journals

The Times of India, New Delhi.

Economic and Political Weekly, Mumbai.

Islam and Muslim Societies, Serial Publications, New Delhi.

The Eastern Anthropologist. Serial Publication, New Delhi.

Index

H

I